love,
Dad

love, Dad

LETTERS OF FAITH TO MY CHILDREN

Herbert Brokering

Augsburg
MINNEAPOLIS

To my mother
Clara Marie Utz Brokering
and my father
Heinrich Friedrich Ludwig Brokering
who gave me the time of my life.

LOVE, DAD
Letters of Faith to My Children

Copyright © 1998 Augsburg Fortress. All rights reserved. Except for brief quotations in critical articles or reviews, no part of this book may be reproduced without prior written permission from the publisher. Write to: Permissions, Augsburg Fortress, Box 1209, Minneapolis, MN 55440.

Cover design: David Meyer
Interior design: Elizabeth Boyce

Library of Congress Cataloging-in-Publication Data
Brokering, Herbert F.
    Love, Dad: letters of faith to my children / Herbert F.
Brokering.
        p. cm.
    Includes bibliographical references.
    ISBN 0-8066-3619-X (alk. paper)
    1. Christian life—Lutheran authors.   2. Brokering, Herbert F.
I. Title.
BV4501.2.B758   1998   98-9577
248.4'841—dc21   CIP

The paper used in this publication meets the minimum requirements of American National Standard for Information Sciences—Permanence of Paper for Printed Library Materials, ANSI Z329.48-1984.   ∞

Manufactured in the U.S.A.   AF 9-3619

04   2   3   4   5   6   7   8

Contents

Family Legacies—An Introduction

My family today: children—Mark, born in 1952; Beth, 1954; Jon, 1956; and Chris, 1958; their mother, my wife—Lois, 1929.

My childhood family: siblings—Paul, born in 1917; Louisa, 1921; Harold, 1924; Herbert, 1926; Gertrude, 1928; parents—Clara Marie Utz Brokering, born in 1893; Heinrich Friedrich Ludwig Brokering, 1883.

Love, Dad is a collection of letters to my children. The letters are a scrapbook from my life of seventy years. They are my history, my passion, my memoirs—my *love* for you, my children. These letters are also my legacy of faith to you—God's faith in me, God's faith in us. God believes in me, I believe in this believing and faithful God. That is the bottom line of the letters.

The letters are written first of all to you, my children, Mark, Beth, Jon, Chris. They are also for your families and friends and for the children you, too, will know; because these letters are important parts of your histories, passions, and faith, as well as mine. And the letters are for all those who have passed on to you God's faithfulness, in ways known and not. You've heard that it takes a village to raise a child. It took heaven and earth to raise you: angels, uncles, aunts, baby-sitters, saints, neighbors, teachers, classmates, lovers, heroes.

Finally, I write these letters for all who have fathers, are fathers, will be fathers—for all who raise the children of the world. They speak of God's goodness to all the earth, to all fathers and children, to the universe.

I was not a perfect father. I did not always listen, or look with fatherly care at what you'd done, or offer you good choices, or feel your hurts, or model faith. But I have always liked being your dad; I like what we did together. The more I remembered as I wrote these letters, the more thankful I was for the chance to be your father.

My father was not perfect either. But I am not a victim of his failures. I do not wallow in the mistakes from my childhood. It took me many years to embrace the mistakes, forgive the hurts, and go on with life empowered. But this has been done. I like who I am now. I hope you will do the same with the shortcomings and hurt from your childhood. Do not stay a victim of a father's failures. Ride the world, keep your passion, believe God, have fun along the way.

My father left me a rich legacy of faith in the words he spoke, in the letters he wrote. When I went off to college, he wrote me often. His letters were long, typed, and detailed, like those he sent to his family in Europe. I did not write home often. Looking back, I know they waited for letters from me that never came. And now I regret my failure.

I wish I'd had more time to ask my own father questions, to hear his stories and tell him mine. I wish I'd taken the time to go walking with him, visit his European homestead with him, sit in comfortable silence with him. I wish I'd taken more time to tell my dad I love him. I would thank my father, feel his hurt and his joy, ask about his growing up. I would ask him about his mother and father. We didn't take enough time to share our lives with each other.

Perhaps that is why I am writing these letters to you.

Love, Dad could not have been written without a loving mom. Your mother was always there for you. She filled in when I was gone. She shielded you, cheered you on, kept you safe, heard your stories, kissed your wounds, talked with you about God, took you to every club and school group you joined. She made me a better father to you. Our roles overlapped. Sometimes she did Dad things, and I did Mom things. I liked making you pancakes shaped like animals; she liked gardening. You all learned to sew, swing a hammer, make beds, do laundry, and cook. Sometimes you played Dad, and I learned from you.

The letters are grouped into five sections or themes. The sections express discoveries, insights, hopes, and assurances all fathers wish to share with their children: *Here's a place you'll like; There's someone I want you to meet; Have fun along the way; I know the feeling; and I have faith in you.*

It is my hope that these letters will kindle old memories, new stories, and closer bonds among all fathers and children who read them. I hope, too, that the letters will inspire you to share legacies of faith and love with your own children, with your own parents. You have stories, memories, experiences, passions that are vital parts of your family's history. Share these with one another. Make time for storytelling—in extended family groups, around the dinner table, or in quiet corners by the fire. Preserve your stories and memories in gifts of Christmas letters, in birthday cards, on the backs of family photos, on pages of scrapbooks and albums. Gather family members around a tape recorder and capture recollections and stories that have enriched your home through the years.

In all your stories and letters, speak of the faith that binds your family together in spite of their differences, their disappointments, their failures—the faith that binds each of you to a larger, more ancient family, one that will go on forever.

Love,

Herb Brokering

Herbert Brokering, Father and Son

*Here's a place
you'll like.*

When you were little, home was in the valley along the Minnesota River.
You came with swamp mud and joyful stories to the front door,
and you were home. The house was your home; so was the valley.
Home became places you learned by heart,
places that made you welcome.

Your Home Place

Go to the place or places where you have your peace.

When you were little, home was in the valley along the Minnesota River. You came with swamp mud and joyful stories to the front door, and you were home. The house was your home; so was the valley. As you grew older, home became places you learned by heart, places that made you welcome. Sometimes a friend's house seemed more like home than our front door. You liked going there, being there, eating and staying over.

Hitchhiking home from college was for me a high, holy time. It was a way for me to look at home as a distant, sacred place. I usually hitched alone, taking whatever rides came to me. I risked safety, stood in dust on highways, waited hours for a ride, rode anything going toward home. The last miles were often walked through the dark, hearing farm dogs bark, looking for our porch light. I loved school, but that house with its porch light and kitchen table and north bedroom were home. The barn, the one cow, mother's cherry pie, and father's proud eyes were home.

I still move toward places that expect me, love me, offer cherry pie, and have a porch light waiting.

What home did I put inside you? Do you still like a hillside for sledding, a quick prayer before eating, a table around which to play games, a fire in a Franklin stove, a place to show what you wrote and drew and heard during the day?

When I was a boy in Nebraska, we had pigeons that always came back to the same nest. Do you remember how we had raccoons that always returned to our yard? We could tell them by a scar on an ear or a special marking on the tail. Do you still watch the sky for owls and migrant geese; do you still listen for the haunting calls of loons? Are those things part of your home?

The places where we lived have overlapped for me. They are like tells of Jericho, through which I dig to find the layers of our life together. Are my layers your layers? What are the good times that are dear to you? Which ones am I part of, and which will I never know?

Your mother and I have lived where we are for nearly forty years. I think I am saving this homestead to be your place someday. Perhaps you have already inherited it: it is yours through the sacred times of sliding, jumping in leaves, playing hopscotch, marching in parades, and feeding rabbits through the winter. You do none of these now, but they are inside you; and they are what make you cozy, what make you feel at home.

I am really at home when the deepest need inside me is met, when I am quiet, still, balanced. I am home when I have what I need—enough time and space, and no other place to go.

The house is paid for, the wintry hill is steep and white, and the rock garden will soon bloom. Today I am quiet and strong. When I am at home I do not ask God for a single thing more.

Have a good home place. That is what I want most for you.

Love, Dad

A Secret Tree House

When I was a boy, I had a tree house wherever we lived.

It was more than a hideaway. It was a retreat center, a mansion, a castle, a holy of holies. Sometimes it had a ladder I could climb, and others could climb after me. Sometimes it had only a rope, and I was there alone.

I built tree houses with you. They were made of leftover wood; some had railings, some had furniture, some were very simple. I remember trying to climb into one with you. It was too fragile to hold me. It was for you, not for me. Sometimes as you climbed it, I stood below with arms open until you were safe. Once you were in your sanctuary at the top of a Texas tree I felt good. You were in the kind of place you'd always need: a secret tree house.

My dear friend Gerhard Frost often spoke of the private room God gives us all, a secret room that no one else knows about. I liked my tree house—liked the gaps in the floor through which I could peek, liked the vistas I saw in all directions, liked the limbs and leaves touching me so high above the ground.

I have such a tree house now. It's called the Rose Room, and it belongs to us all—you, your mother, me. We built it onto the north end of our house. It rests in oak woods. It has twenty-five windows on walls and ceiling. There are no pictures hanging; each window frames its own masterpiece of nature. I sit inside and feel outside. All seasons pass through the window frames. Cardinals, pheasants, deer, sparrows, finches, mallards, raccoons, squirrels touch us on all sides. I can see stars and dippers framed in ten ceiling windows. I know exactly where the November moon is at seven P.M. and at four in the morning. It is my tree house. And inside that house I have a simpler secret place—a sanctuary I can enter at any time.

Find your own tree house, your own sanctuary. Keep it simple: a place that fits your soul, a place to be when traffic is too heavy and talk is too loud. It is your little bit of heaven, a few rungs higher than your earth.

I call my tree house the Rose Room because a miniature rose lives there. When you were little, we named places, rocks, animals, trees. We knew them by their names; we made them special with names. Names make things special. Name your tree house. Name your sanctuary. Make it that special. It's all right to keep the name a secret, nobody else needs to know. Some secrets make being human special.

So do secret sanctuaries.

Love, Dad

Spaces Between

Do you remember times in the dark room?

The joy of negative and positive space unfolding in the warm liquid of a yellow developing pan? Seeing things in an opposite way—blond hair a dark shadow, tee shirts and teeth black? It was like hearing a sentence inside out, seeing a tree through the dark, reading words upside down, listening to what is not said aloud. This stirred our imagination.

What I liked most of all was to see a photo slowly appear within a blank sheet of paper. Sometimes we developed film that was months old, wondering what we'd shot. It was a secret. I have a roll of film from years ago that we have not yet developed. I wonder if the picture is still there. I almost like not knowing, yet imagining.

It is good to read silence, notice a hush or a flinch in a face, look between lines, hear the unsaid. This is thinking space, distance for figuring yourself out, time for filling blank lines in large pages.

Do you enjoy negative spaces? Do you notice shapes, spaces between, sizes, dimensions, hues?

When I was teaching seminarians we slowly moved through the spaces between chairs, tables, benches, and furniture that made up many learning centers. We focused on useful spaces for learning. We thought of ways to use this space differently to make learning flexible, beautiful, fun. We moved furniture to fit learning themes, we made our bodies fit a subject matter.

This is also how we arranged your rooms in our home. Often we changed room spaces late in the night. The changes determined not so much how the room looked, but rather how we might live differently in the new arrangement. A friend once commented, "I don't like your furniture, but I like the spaces between it." Our basement went through many shifts and changes in forty

years. The rooms in which we sleep and study are always chang-
ing. Space is a gift of God, and how we see a place and enjoy it is
a game we are given to play.

Life is full of spaces, shapes, directions, and each has its own
purpose.

I once had graduate students feel spaces under desks, memorize them with their hands and imaginations—and then not look
at them at all. The spaces once unknown now fascinated them.
They wanted to look; some did peek, I am certain. Their flat
worlds suddenly took on dimensions and mystery; spaces grew in
all directions, up and down, inside, outside, sideways.

Space is your gift. It has given you times of life: days, moments,
years; it has given you today. Space makes up your expectation—
what's around the corner, what you have placed safe inside, what
you will unravel in your next conversation. Space is where you
hoard and cherish values.

When we are all eating together from one loaf and drinking
from one cup, our life grows larger, our love closer, our memories
longer. Space around the family table was important in your growing up. It is still important.

A dark room is not so dark when the negative begins to unfold.
Sometimes a whole world opens up in negative space.

Love, Dad

A Good Rocking Chair

I have three rocking chairs.

Hardly a day ends without me rocking. As I rock I look north, I look up, I look in, I look back; I see over some distant mountain. I rock myself in all directions.

We rocked you when you were little. An unfinished rocker was our first new exciting furniture. We painted it green. O how we held you when we rocked you. You clung to us, we rocked each other.

I know my mother rocked me. She must have hummed songs into me and breathed her warm free spirit over me. In graduate school I studied how low IQs were raised through rocking, holding, hugging, touching. It's always been true.

I like the picture in this old blessing: "The Lord lift his countenance upon you, and give you peace." I rocked you with my countenance, with my whole being. That's how I have been rocked through life—with compassion, under God's whole countenance. I pretend God has a rocker.

I believe rocking is part of us all. It is how we stayed alive in our mother. Nine months we rocked. Rocking is the story of Noah's family in the flood. They rocked and rocked, forty days and nights and more inside the ark. The storm outside, the wind, the rain, the danger; and inside the womb of the ark they rocked, ate and drank, rocked, stayed alive and well, rocked. This ancient Bible story is about being safe.

Moses was a national hero; he led Israel to a promised land. He was rocked in a basket, in water filled with bulrushes. There the daughter of Pharaoh found him, rescued him, raised him; and he led millions in a freedom march.

I like seeing babies cuddled in the arms of a parent. How often they rock together—mother and child rocking, father and baby rocking. At a daughter's wedding, a father dances with his child. It is like rocking. At a family funeral, a mother hugs her daughter, a father hugs his son; they move together in grief. They rock each other. That must be what we learn inside a mother, rocking, dancing, rhythm.

There are stormy days when it's best to rock and wait, to find a metronome of movement that soothes.

I sit in the plains of Minnesota and rock, and I feel the tides off San Francisco, the beat of waves off the Sea of Japan. Then I am with you and with the universe. I rock and watch the old moon move slowly across winter skies, through early summer mornings, and I am with you. I turn my rocker in the directions where you live; I rock facing you, and we are together.

Sometimes you went with me to the salvage dump. Do you remember when we rescued a grandma rocking chair? It sets low, rocks slow and easy. It's like riding a slow pony. We removed seven coats of paint and set the chair in the yard under the sun. I said, "Sun, this is the tree you once grew. Chair, this is the sun you once knew." They met again. We placed the rocker on a patio, in many positions, and took pictures of rocking-chair shadows. Beautiful. A friend wove a hemp seat into the chair. You liked rocking in it.

No babies are alike. No rocking is the same. I think we rocked each of you differently. I have three rocking chairs; each rocks me differently. I feel held when I rock in them.

Love, Dad

Souvenir Room

My study has always had mementos, souvenirs.

You called them "Dad's stuff." Your friends came to see. Hundreds of stories are stored there. I brought graduate students to the room. We sat and talked for hours, looking at six-year-old apple cores that are nearly dust, a feather quill from a movie filmed with Roland Bainton, a leaf mark you printed into plaster of Paris. The leaf is gone, but the leaf print is there, your fingerprints are there. The friends who ate the apples are gone, but their story lives on. The film is finished and Bainton is buried, but men and women come to meet him in my goose quill. We laugh at his cartoons of life, his quips, his humor. I tell them how he sometimes prayed looking up, winking in prayer. He was not afraid of God. One feather and all this memory.

My study is more than a mess. I muse here. It's my museum.

Last week Tom, eleven years old, and I were together for two hours. I was helping him finish a Scout church project. We spent ninety minutes in one room just looking at what was there, looking for stories, images with meaning. We talked about what he saw, what I saw. We scribbled down each sight, each word of the other. I have my journey book; he has his. Sometime I will tell you details of my two hours with Tom and a room full of mementos. I am seventy; he is eleven. It was like being with Jesus, age twelve, in the temple.

Tom's mind is like that room—full, a museum. You are that way.

The Rose Room has twenty-five windows. Windows frame creation paintings: oak trees, sky, tips of blossoms, stars, deer, pheasants, tulips standing straight, a blooming crabapple, willow branches, rain on glass, frost, Kenny planting tomatoes, Carol raking autumn leaves, Lois in the rock garden, geese flying north. A treasure house. A room filled with souvenirs.

When things collect, pile up, there comes the chance to see them anew. Everything overlaps, everything touches. Going through old things forms new connections. Songs are born out of mementos touching, souvenirs overlapping, thoughts connecting. We have the chance to bring new order to chaos. A gift.

The world is made of overlays. What looks like a mess may be layers of life. Archaeological digs uncover layers of history, bring the past to the present. The mind is a tell, filled with levels of living, past and present.

In time we let go of souvenirs and mementos. Last year you helped put some of "Dad's stuff" into a dumpster, back in the earth. They are gone. Now I am writing more, savoring new things, making stories, waking a power in me. My cup is full, overflowing.

Mementos, souvenirs. Past and present. Life is layers.

Love, Dad

Lake Superior in Ice

I like ice cream on Sundays.

We are visiting the north shore of Lake Superior. April ice is breaking. You know this shore. I am overwhelmed with the ice cracking, turning, pushing, pulling, piling up, drifting back to sea.

When I was little in Nebraska we cracked winter ice in the creek, stuffed chunks into a gunny sack, pounded the ice until it was in fine pieces. Then we poured it around an aluminum tub set inside a wooden ice bucket. With milk, eggs, and vanilla we made ice cream — a Sunday evening winter ritual. Sunday-night ice cream made Sunday-morning going to church even better. It kept the whole day holier. Ice cream was our Sunday winter ritual in Humboldt, Nebraska.

I liked cracking the ice for that ice cream.

Today, sixty years after those winter boyhood Sundays, I watch the ice pounding the shores of Lake Superior. As winter grows colder, waters of the great lake grow quiet. The February sea is silent. Dashing waves are stilled by deep cold. Waves churn deep inside, under heavy ice; we cannot see them. But in April the ice is broken into a million pieces, like my childhood Sunday creek. Like a wintry jigsaw puzzle.

Pieces of that wintry puzzle are loosened, scattered, refrozen into a pattern my mother would have wanted in a homemade quilt.

Wind and tides sculpt castles, ice landscapes that dance in the sun. White gulls know a waking sea will soon give back their daily fish. On peaks of ice, birds sing sacred supper songs.

I was nine years old. We crushed creek ice in a gunny sack — an awesome sound. Sixty years later I hear wind and waves crush ice masses to rouse a sleeping sea. Awesome dawning. Winter will let go.

Suddenly an April snowstorm floods the lake of broken ice. Wind and snow hit my face, my hair, my hands with meaning. I know a feeling from years before. And I am hungry for ice cream.

We ate ice cream in a warm kitchen, sitting around a tan enameled table, both flaps up. I with a Charlie McCarthy spoon, my brother with a Kaiser Wilhelm spoon—my father's souvenir from immigrating in 1906.

I am famished for ice cream standing in the blowing snow.

A sudden white-out thrills me. I remember words from a psalm and I say them aloud: "Praise the Lord from the earth . . . all deeps, fire and hail, snow and frost, stormy wind fulfilling his command! . . . Praise the Lord."

Slipping on new snow, my feet find the shoreline, the rocks. I hunch down and hunt stones worn smooth from tides. My hands are cold, as they were when I cracked ice at the creek. I find two red rocks, souvenirs—wintry red roses. I clutch them and climb an embankment to the road.

Winter roses, these rocks. Years have worn them small. But what they are from their beginning is still inside them. Young years are in them.

Youth is still in us. The child making Sunday ice cream lives. I hear ice smashing, I taste vanilla ice cream.

Love, Dad

Night Playground

Do you still love the night?

When nights are long, I remember how you played in the dark.

I, too, played in the night as a child. Under a strong country yard light, I ran in and out of darkness with my sisters and brother. When I played with friends in the dark, I felt even more safe.

Wonderful night. I could hide in the dark and wait to be found there. I could smile inside a safe, dark hiding place. If it was too light, we were found too soon. The more I feared the dark, the more it intrigued me to play there. And the more I came to love it.

You also loved the night. I liked when you played in the dark. Sometimes, though, I feared your nights; I cared how safe you were. I often watched over you, and you did not know it.

In the dark it's hard to tell people from shadows. Darkness plays tricks. When the darkness was deep, the game was harder, we ran faster, hid more silently. When it was very dark we could hear ourselves breathing. I heard your voices grow stronger as darkness increased, as though you had to shout louder to cut the night—perhaps to feel safer.

Now when it's dark and I cannot sleep, I can still hear you outside at play. For a time as a grownup, I feared the night. I do not fear it now. I have learned again to play in the dark.

You lived in a river valley, on a dead-end street with no streetlights. You knew bright stars that were not washed out by city lights. You saw stars fall like burning streaks. You saw fireflies sparkle a night sky. You saw fireworks miles away decorating a deep purple sky. You saw lightning break a black sky into pieces. You saw rainbows span the twilight valley after storms. You liked when night closed your eyes in sleep. Night is a friend.

When lights went out we spoke our night wishes. We imagined in the dark. We wondered how it would be to sit beside an owl and hoot in darkness. We wished to follow a cat through a night to find what it knows about dark silence, dark sounds, all-night feelings.

Sometimes we woke with you in the night and looked at long fingers of shadow stretching over the yard. Now when I wake, shadows seem even stronger, night seems more real, more awesome. I sometimes go to sit between shadows and feel the shade of oak trees in moonlight. Night shadows are more silent. The moon gives a different kind of shade.

Sometimes we learned by making night shadows. I remember being playful with you, doing theater on an asphalt parking lot under a streetlight. Our bodies danced stories in shadows. We loved night.

Tonight I walked in the dark to see robins sleep, to find out if violets close, to feel shadows of maple leaves, to hear a willow whisper and bow in the wind. Someone on a riverboat is working a night shift, talking loudly into the dark waters below our house.

I imagine night nurses stepping softly in and out of rooms. I see red eternal candles bright in dark cathedrals. The Milky Way reads like a miracle when I study it.

I remember a night-light we left burning in your bedroom forty years ago.

Tonight I walked in the dark. I played that you were looking for me, would find me. We ran and laughed and you touched me. So now I'm "it." Tonight I'm "it." It's your turn to hide, and I'll look for you. I'm your father; I will look for you.

Love, Dad

Sacred Places

How do we make a place more sacred?

How can a place we know well be made more special? I told
you stories of the Bible, so you might know they were true today. I
drew pictures of the Holy Land in the earth and marked sites with
stones so you'd feel how near we live to God. I mentioned Omaha,
Minneapolis, Duluth, San Francisco, and Tokyo along with
Jerusalem and Bethlehem in my poems and hymns. I hoped we'd
know God is as real here as in those ancient Bible cities. We played
and prayed this way. I write this way. I believe this way.

While my brother went to the Holy Land and walked in the
Jordan River, I drove to Nebraska and stood in a creek. I waded
in water in a place important since my childhood. I looked into
the creek water and said, "You came from springs of Banias,
north of Galilee; you fed the Jordan River where Jesus stood." I
thought of my brother standing in the Jordan the same day; and
I faced east and said, "You are standing in water from Nebraska,
from our childhood. I am in the Jordan water in this Nebraska
creek."

How quickly places can cross to touch and bless each other.

You stood with us around two candles in the snow. The candle
flames were bright as wintry stars. We watched shadows from the
light on the sparkling snow. We called the place Bethlehem; it was
northern Minnesota. The two connected on this winter night. The
frozen earth beneath our feet was sacred; we stood in the Holy
Land and felt the joy of Mary and Joseph. You were ten.

Friends came to make a snow grotto in our front yard. Sunrise
came and went. The shape of the grotto changed as the sun rose
higher and days lengthened. The snow melted and froze again,
and nature formed a nativity scene. We marveled. Sometimes a
site needs only a name. Then we see it; it is holy to us.

We played with photographs of friend Sister Noemi. In her photos of dandelions we saw angel feathers over Bethlehem. In ferns unfolding we saw shepherds bending in adoration. In buds bursting we saw children cheering Jesus on a Palm Sunday walk. Our game opened our eyes to new connections.

In a Bible camp I saw a garden of young potatoes. Yellow and white blossoms covered the field. I set a candle and a cross in the center. Children came and admired. They said it was like an altar and these were the altar flowers, blooming. The earth was the first altar, where people made covenants with God.

I have wrapped the story of my brother and me into a parable about sacred places.

Once upon a time
there were those who wanted more than anything
to walk in the water of the Jordan River.
And when they were there,
some stood waist deep
and listened to the sound of the running water.
In the sound of the rushing stream
they could hear the voice of a most warm word, *Beloved.*
They truly felt the warmth
as the water folded around them, *Beloved.*
And they were glad they'd come so far to feel beloved.
Most of the visitors took vials of the Jordan River home,
water in which Jesus himself had stood.
A scientist examined the water
and found it was mostly rain from the state of Oregon.
The water of the Jordan from the days of Jesus
is now in the heart of the U.S.A.
and runs in creeks and rivers of Minnesota and of Iowa.
Yet the visitors agreed it was important to go so far away
to learn of holy places back home.

Next year some of them plan to go
to another part of the world
to see another sacred place
which is in their own home town.
The size of the holy land is increasing.

How quickly a place becomes special. How long it stays sacred
to us. I wish you open eyes to see the holy places that surround you.

Love, Dad

There's someone I want you to meet.

My earliest memories of God were with my mother.
God was about stories she told, picture books we paged through together,
a spirit she had. Mother had a lap. Her apron was like swaddling cloth.
When I sat in her lap, she sometimes wrapped her apron around me,
and I was in a nest, a manger. My earliest image of heaven is my mother.

Good Teachers

Throughout my school years I couldn't wait to meet my teachers.

From country elementary schools through several graduate schools, I do not recall a bad teacher. They were different, each teacher like one piece of a great puzzle. And it was up to me to fit the pieces together for learning.

We talked about your teachers, met them, counseled with them through the years, thanked them, and sometimes took them to task. I envied the amount of your lives they spent with you, and the topics and feelings you shared with them—things I never knew about. They represented your parents, and in some ways they represented God to you. They were the guardians of your mind, of your future.

Some challenged you when you threw a square pot on a round potter's wheel, and you learned with them that you were unique, an inventor. Some drove you to practice for perfection; with them you reached your outer limits. Some became a best friend, and you learned to emulate a great mind, a compassionate heart. Some taught you to argue inside yourself and to look at everything from many sides—like Picasso, and your spirit grew. Some were a trial for you; through them, too, you discovered who you are.

You have remembered all of them. Some you have thanked.

Do you remember my stories about the professor who taught me that a word is a world? I was nineteen then, and his course was called "Form Criticism." Thirty-five years later, I read that he'd died. I wrote his widow a letter telling her of my thanks and admiration for this great mentor. I poured out gratitude as to a best friend. I also thanked her for her father, another professor, who that same year had taught me a course on the life of Christ. He was tall and gentle, and he leaned over us with love when he talked about Jesus. He taught as though he were an eyewitness, as though he had walked those ancient Judean roads, Galilean hillsides and deserts himself. I thanked her for her father's reverent imagination. It felt good to give thanks for these teachers.

Thirty years ago I began teaching courses of Creative Education in seminaries. Students are now writing me, remembering when we sat on teeter-totters and spoke words that balanced, recalling how we walked downtown by twos with eyes closed to learn trust. We loved learning together. Everyone got a passing grade.

You remember teachers by name. I remember Mr. Hertel. He recruited me for college—not to play football or for a scholarship, just to go to Wartburg College in Iowa. He drove 300 miles to our country parsonage and asked me to come to his college. We could not afford college, but he said I could earn my way by washing dishes, waiting tables, raking leaves, washing windows and walls. That is what I did, and I often thanked him. He taught biology; coached basketball, baseball, football; and was our dorm master. His eyes were cast down whenever we met him, but in his shy spirit he knew everything about us. When the band played during basketball games, there was one tune we all loved. To the beat of that tune we sang the word "Hertel!" We sang it with love.

I do not remember ever having a bad teacher. I thought they were supposed to be the way they were. There was always something important to learn from each of them. Sometimes it was just to live through the hours of class. That was something good.

So it will always be with those who are teachers, colleagues, friends. All have things to teach, good things.

When we saw the film *The Crucible*, you told me how you directed the play in Tokyo. For two hours we talked about the meaning of this film for America and for students in Japan. I thanked you then. I thank you again in this letter for being my teacher. I thank God for your mind and spirit.

Years pass, our teachers change. We learn from each of them.

Love, Dad

Our Neighbors

Love your neighbor.

For a time we lived in a Jewish community in Long Island, New York. Two of you were born there. It was for me a first long visit to the Holy Land. It was there I met tradition, the Torah, Seders, Passover. There I heard about Hanukkah and the Maccabees and began visits with Rabbi Sandrow who invited me to preach in his synagogue.

Your Jewish pediatrician was like a rabbi. He taught us when he healed you. Our neighbors invited us to their holy days and we saw them redeem firstborn sons in ceremonies. We witnessed a Cohen, from the tribe of Levi, buy back his firstborn son from God. Each firstborn son of Israel is God's at birth. With prayers, ceremony, offerings, and a sacred covenant, the boy becomes a full member of the Jewish family. There was a band playing and there was wine. What a festival. These were your neighbors.

Can you remember the excitement of Jewish holy days?

On Christmas Eve a fifth of our congregation was made up of Jewish neighbors. They liked the story of this Jewish family of Jesus, they liked the mystical mass, the music with candlelight, the glow on our faces. They knew stories of God's glory. They understood old Simeon and Anna who looked for salvation in the temple.

They knew of evil Herod who waged war on Bethlehem's children. They knew of holocaust and prejudice. And they knew of peace. They wanted to discuss what we knew and believed.

Rabbis came each year to our congregation to show us their Sabbath, the festival of their Passover, and to wear phylacteries to connect head, heart, and hand with love. I savored these times and captured the rabbis' words on old tape reels. How many are the wonderful pieces of life's puzzle. Who could ever be bored with life, neighbors, other lands?

You were very little—some weren't born yet—when we lived with Jewish neighbors. I sat in their temples on Friday nights and heard cantors sing prayers and songs about God the Rock. They asked me to preach seven times in their synagogues. I did, and Swedish, German, and Norwegian members of my parish sat among them. They wanted to hear about Jesus, to know what we said about his words and deeds. They listened to every word. Once we stayed afterwards and talked for two hours about Christians throwing stones at Jews in Brooklyn.

That was forty years ago. Do you know Jewish people now?

Years later I wrote a book, *In a Promise*. It is a collection of Old Testament poetry set to photography by Benedictine Sister Noemi of Duluth. I dedicated the book to Rabbi Sandrow and later took it to him in Long Island. He had died two years earlier. I left the book with his family and explained my gratitude. I feel he heard my words and likes the book.

What a world God gives us to know, to visit, to cheer, to invite for dinner, to join in silence or prayer. I close my letter with an old Jewish question I asked long ago in Long Island, and still ask: "Who is my neighbor?"

Love, Dad

People of God

How did you grow to who you are? How did you become the person you like being?

I often sit in a favorite rocking chair and think about how God grew in me. It began in Nebraska where people loved me. They were hardworking farmers, Lutherans, members of our country parish. They spoke German or English. If it was a kind of ghetto, it was also home. God lived there. Everyone I knew went to church.

When I was very little, Mother gave me a picture of a missionary with a great white beard holding hands with a native child of New Guinea. I memorized their names. During the week I kept this tiny picture in a secret drawer so it would not be lost. On Sundays I carried it in my white shirt pocket and looked at it often while my father preached. I began to think of New Guinea, somewhere beyond Nebraska. God liked other countries, too.

Once a year we drove to Omaha, slowing down as we passed Boys' Town. I knew the name Father Flannagan, and I'd heard that the boys there were probably Catholic, that they had been bad and the father helped make them good again. I later learned that you didn't have to be Catholic to be bad — or to get into Boys' Town. My world grew, and I discovered there were good people other than Lutherans. I learned Catholics, too, were religious and knew God.

Have I told you these stories? How did God grow real to you?

My father taught me that in Holy Communion, the broken bread gets to be more than bread; it is a whole feast. You don't have to eat a lot, the way you do at suppertime, in this feast. A little bit is all we need, and we're present at a table big enough for all people on earth. Father taught that saints and angels attend the Holy Eucharist. I began to see the church as global. And God grew.

A Methodist classmate rode with me to high school. He was kinder than many of my Lutheran school friends, and he knew more songs by heart than we did. My world of music and love increased. God spoke through music and Methodists.

College was far away, 300 miles. We were not allowed to dance at Wartburg College, and I sometimes sneaked off to a Baptist church to hear them clap hands, watch them dance and wave arms, hear them sing songs about the power of the blood of God. God was a spirit and spirits could dance.

Do you sit and rock, or take a slow walk, and think of how your faith grew?

At the age of nineteen, I was a graduate student at the University of Iowa, and my roommate was an atheist. He looked at my catechism, which I had taken with me. We talked about important things, ate together, laughed, helped each other with Statistics. He became a dear friend. My world grew. I no longer thought only of Lutherans and Christians.

God knows the language of the secular and sacred. All is sacred with God.

Have I told you these things? These are some of my God stories. Now I want to hear your stories of God. They will not be like mine.

Love, Dad

Someone to Help Push

It's a kind world.

Today did not go as planned. I could have said it was a bummer. But it was a day of kindness. The cup is full.

You know I bought an old Buick because I felt admiration for it being old and still doing well. That was about the time I received my retirement pin, which I returned. There must be better ways— ways to give the old empowering words and responsibility. I know older persons who now are truly ready to do their life's work with wisdom and authority. These feelings nudged me to buy the blue Buick Century on the spot, and to name it after a song I loved in the Forties, "Blue Bird of Happiness."

It's been a snowy winter in Minnesota. While seeing editors about this book, I parked on Fifth Avenue. After a visit in the book department, I could not move Blue Bird from the parking spot. One back wheel spun, the other was frozen. Smokers standing outside the *Star and Tribune* building watched and smoked on, as did my tire. I rocked, spun, prayed, and stayed stuck at the curb.

This was the day after O. J. Simpson was found guilty in a second court trial. Newscasters talked about tensions between races, and attitudes of blacks and whites were aired on talk shows.

A man came to my car door to ask if he could help. He pushed and pushed and grew tired in his white shirt and good suit. Then someone helped him; but the car stayed at the curb, the hole in the ice grew deeper. They excused themselves to go back to work. I rocked Blue Bird and prayed and talked to her kindly. I did not know what was wrong, that a brake had frozen. The emergency brake had not been used for years, and rust had set in. Accidentally I had stepped on the emergency pedal when I parked. The brake froze.

An African-American man came to my car door and asked to help. He told me not to gun the engine. He kept saying in a soft voice as he pushed, "Walk it slowly like walking a dog." He got in and tried to walk it like a dog, but Blue Bird stayed spinning at the curb. Then four men were pushing my car while he tried walking it like a dog. Blue Bird did not walk. He got out and whispered to me, "You walk it, and I'll help push."

Five men pushed, the frozen brake released, the wheel turned. I rode off waving, waving, thumb up and praising.

Sometimes just walk it and let someone help push.

Still not knowing about the frozen brake, I parked myself into another corner at the Fireside Pizza Cafe, ten miles from home. Kevin, a friend, came with a yellow cloth to kneel on. He saw the problem, then jacked up the car and used the few tools in my trunk to try loosening the brake. My tools were too fragile. He needed a sledge hammer. I watched him spend his lunch break on his knees—an act of worship. To worship means "to do your work before God." This had been a day of worship.

I phoned a tow truck and waited two hours. Joe arrived looking as though he'd rather get Blue Bird going than do anything else in the world. He asked important questions, as would my doctor. He hoisted the rear wheels, crawled underneath, lay in the snow, and took a huge hammer to the frozen brake. The hammer was mighty, rust flew in all directions, Bluebird was released.

I rode away waving, singing, feeling released. At home, I immediately phoned Kevin: "You're a genius. You did everything right. My tools were too weak. You only needed the big hammer." He felt the hour on his knees well spent, I could tell in his laughter.

The day did not go as planned. Today I feel a kindness in this world. The news is filled with racial tensions. Stereotypes were reshaped in me today. I see the men pushing; I hear the words "Walk it like a dog." I see my friend on his knees to help. It was such a good day—so different, not spoiled. Different than I had planned. Good enough to write you about.

Love, Dad

Heroes within Us

People are tucked inside us.

I have Nebraska heroes living inside me forever. They are friends, neighbors from my childhood. They have died; they live in me like heroes. They make me glad for my life.

Mr. Haecker gave me trust. He let me run a combine and tractor for long hours over rough fields. He smiled when he fixed chains I broke, then showed me how to cross deep washouts without tipping the tractor or breaking chains.

Mr. Spilker filled me with pride. He plowed a perfect field; his rows were straight. One day he got off the tractor and said softly so I could hardly hear: "You plow this field." I could hardly believe it. He helped me plow the center row straight. Then I plowed the field around that line. Sunday at church, farmers knew I had done the field. I was overflowing with pride.

For thirty minutes on New Year's Eve I rang the old year out, the new year in. Being alone at midnight in a cold, country church was awesome. On that hill a whole year left, a whole year began. The ringing told the countryside the news of New Year. While Guy Lombardo played in New York, I rang a bell in Pickerell. One-half mile south of church, Mrs. Hertlein turned on her yard light at midnight. Each year it was so. I know she knew I was there. I think of her often when I want to be brave.

Mrs. Doetker cooked the best chicken for thrashers. I was the water boy; I washed last under the tree before lunchtime. She gave me a clean white towel. Fourteen men and I sat around the big table, potatoes and chicken steaming on platters. No one took a bite until Mrs. Doetker prayed. The way Mrs. Doetker prayed with those men is tucked in me.

Old Mr. Craemer had deep face wrinkles, his mustache was long and stained with smoke. He drove fast and braked hard when he stopped before our house on Monday mornings. Dust settled.

He came to talk with my father about Sunday's sermon. I never listened in. I liked that Mr. Craemer thought the sermon was worth discussing. I knew how many, many hours my father had studied and practiced to preach. Mr. Craemer comes to mind whenever I listen to preaching.

Mrs. Hoefling limped. I think she had polio. Her daughter limped, too; I think she also had polio. I was lucky not to have caught it. Like the Black Plague it crept through our countryside. I admired Mrs. Hoefling. She was quiet, smiled, and never looked like limping made her unhappy. She didn't stay away from things because she walked differently from other women. I think of her when my body hurts, and when I have to go somewhere in public hurting.

Leonard lived one mile north. He fixed things and was kind. He was a few years older than I and helped Father do what we were not strong enough or skilled enough to do. He came over and asked, "How can I help?" Leonard's farm was not neat, but he was. I never saw his mother in church, but Leonard came, and he always came early. He seems very old now. He smiles the same as then, and would still fix anything I asked, if it needed a hammer or a welding torch or a smile. Why do I think of him often, when I have only seen him twice in the past fifty years?

Loretta was my country school teacher. Her spelling was not perfect and I don't remember if her punctuation was always correct. I hardly remember anything she taught. She moved among us like the Holy Spirit. She made all the space between us feel good so we could learn from one another. My writing still looks like Loretta's, and I need an editor or the spell check. But I think of Loretta a lot when I read, imagine, write.

You have not met these heroes of mine. They lived a few miles from my country home. They shaped my life. Who are the people you admire? Tell me about them.

Love, Dad

Grandma with the Good Heart

Respect for others is a virtue. So is self-respect.

For a while you had a grandma—Grandma Redelfs, your mother's mother. You honored her from the heart. She loved you, praised you, adored you. She gave you the gift of respect.

We memorized her words, her clichés; we laughed when she repeated proverbs, her bits of wisdom. We smiled when she felt good about her judgment and when her word made a difference. When times were hard, she prayed. The power of her silent words made us safer than before. She prayed when all was well. Remember how she spoke to God aloud at mealtimes? Her body straightened, her face looked toward a holy city, into some bright light. She spoke with words she saved for such times. We learned honor and reverence in her prayers, which were told straight to God. There was no one between her and the Holy One. She was not afraid; she was full of reverence.

From her, you learned to honor. Grandma Redelfs left us, and she left a legacy. What we did alongside Grandma we could now do with others who were older in years. I think of Russ. For years Russ sold us insurance, and after each of his house calls we felt safer. He made sure we had the best policy year by year. Russ talked about each of us as if we were important, shook our hands, promised to be back. We were his young friends; he was like Grandma—older. He became a closer relative when his family separated. We listened to him when others turned away. He remembered the good times with us, reviewed our family stories, asked how each one was. He kept us in his heart. We felt respect for each other.

It was leftover respect from Grandma days. We heard Russ's feelings, saw his rashes, his shortness of breath, and noticed when he drove more slowly. We encouraged his walking, exercising, eating good food. We loaned him books to read. He came when there were birthdays, took us to restaurants as he had twenty years before. He dropped more and more food onto his tie, his eyelids grew heavy in the middle of a sentence. He talked about God with reverence and had new questions about faith, about life. There were repetitions and gaps in his speech. He laughed and joked with us. He forgot his phone number.

When Grandma's eyes dimmed and her mind faded, we went for her heart. We visited those around her in a nursing home. You ad-libbed with Esther who spoke freely inside her Alzheimer illness. When Esther's thoughts were broken, you went for her heart. Her spirit jumped for joy when she recognized you coming off the elevator. You showed her respect.

I am older. I am not dropping my food on my tie, and I am not forgetting my phone number. But I am older, and I believe you are noticing this. We are all growing, and growing older. Older is different for each of us. Now we do what we did not do before.

Notice when I am growing, *how* I am growing—not only older. Notice my new feelings. Tell me your dreams, ask my opinion on a novel idea. Grant me a wish, wink sometimes. Mention when you notice something special about me. Recite something we once knew by heart. Laugh about a time that I am sorry happened. Build me a rail on stairs before I need it. I will use it gradually—when the time comes, when no one is looking. If such a day comes, walk slower so I do not trail behind you. Tell me a good thing I did with you that you will always remember. Ask me if I have a secret I could not tell before. Grab hold of me when either of us is afraid.

Grandma Redelfs went ahead and left you her heart. Someone is always ahead and behind us, giving and receiving respect. Reverence and respect grow from a good heart. Love is the highest gift.

The deer ate the bark off our new apple tree. If they did not eat a complete circle around the trunk, it will live. I will look tomorrow.

Love, Dad

My Mother

My mother left you an inheritance.

You were very young when my mother died. She did not leave you a direct legacy. Let me tell you how you have received my mother's inheritance through me. My mother and I were very close.

She gave me a nest. I liked birds, knew their nesting habits, lived close to them. I thought birds had it good. My mother gave me a good nest, a home, a strong family.

She created a warm space for us. It was not elegant, but it was special. If we were poor, we never felt it. Home was filled with homemade clothes, homemade food, homemade toys. We looked at a Sears catalogue to dream, not buy. Most of what we needed to wear, Mother made. Overalls, socks, and shoes are what we bought; the rest came from Mother. I still hear her sewing machine, see her threading needles with one hand, winding a knot, ready to stitch, darn, sew on buttons. Mother had a thimble, and her fingers were strong with work.

Mother was born a farm girl. She knew how to milk cows, cold pack food, care for gardens, and separate milk and cream. I don't know anything Mother could not do, inside the house or outside.

She approached us slowly. Her actions were never quick, unless we were in danger. She was patient with us all, not pushing, not pulling. She was there, alongside us, making sure we weren't alone. Mother always seemed close by, and close to God.

Sometimes Mother was alone in a world I wanted to know. She looked into space to see something that I knew was hers only. I wished to be there with her. She gave me hope; she helped me believe in a world invisible. She looked farther than eyes can see.

Mother fed us good food. She made food special, and it was always prayed over before eaten. She worked with dough to make bread, rolls, pies. She decorated pie crusts and pressed patterns into homemade butter. There was not anything we would not eat if Mother made it. Buttermilk soup was sweeter with raisins. When her hot pads were worn, we made new ones with her. She helped us help her. Taking turns with her, we shook a jar to make butter, cranked ice cream, sliced noodles on a board, cleaned chickens for cooking. We did these things because she did them, and we were there with Mother.

Being in her kitchen was an honor. Shaking rugs and making them snap was a privilege. Darning socks with her meant we were in the same room, talking softly about something we each knew.

On Mother's Day we picked white flowers from springtime bushes and gave them to Mother. She would wear them to church and tell us of her mother, who died when she was very little. Mother savored family connections.

Mother helped us feel good when our world was too adult. She helped us fold hankies into cloth toys, make dolls from marigolds, draw faces and cartoons. She knew when I was drawing pictures of deer and ships and Joe Louis. It was quiet when I drew pictures and she stitched a quilt set up in the parlor. We talked while I dried dishes, and I can see her fingers wrinkled from warm dishwater. Her fingers were strong and she could ring out clothes like the wringer on our Maytag washer.

She had a big book she read to help us through sickness. I can still smell her medicines—hot tea, honey, and camphor under a warm cotton rag.

Her legs were swollen from standing, and her varicose veins sometimes broke open. Migraine headaches were her woe. I can feel my fingers bringing her relief and can hear her moans that sounded like *Umm* and even like *Amen.*

Mother wrote obituaries of people who died, knew what to say and what to leave out. She didn't want people's feelings hurt. When Paul, my brother, died at eighteen, something changed in her. She still laughed, but the sparkle in her eyes didn't seem to last so long.

I knew she was a wife—my father's wife, but I mostly thought of her as a mother. She knew what to say and when to be still. She looked down sometimes, in order to make peace and to keep joy in the family. She lit a lot of candles and celebrated every holy day. She knew Dad's moods by heart and entered them or escaped them like a dancer.

I never saw Mother run. She hurried, she was on time, she sometimes waited. I never saw Mother run. I never saw her cry. I saw her tears, saw her lips quiver, but I never saw her cry. She held us when we cried. Perhaps she cried along when we did.

Her prayers were simple, and I trusted what she asked for. She talked about angels, and I could feel them in her presence. She seemed always in a prayerful stance. I did not know what a mystic was, nor had I heard of desert fathers. I think your grandmother was a mystic desert mother while she lived inside and all around us five children and Heinrich Brokering, her husband and my father.

My earliest memories of God were with my mother. God was about stories she told, picture books we paged through while I sat in her lap, a spirit she had. Mother's apron was like swaddling cloth. When I sat in her lap, she sometimes wrapped it around me, and I was in a nest, a manger, a sanctuary. My earliest image of heaven is my mother.

Her name was Clara Marie. I braided her waist-long hair. I can still feel her auburn hair against my hands. I can still hear her voice when she told us about her family, her mother who died, and her father who raised her. If you had been older and we had lived closer, you would tell me stories about the words and deeds of your Grandmother Brokering.

I hope you have met your Grandmother Brokering in her son. She wanted me to give you her inheritance.

Love, Dad

44

Your Mother, Lois

We loved, we gave you life.

It is Mother's Day. I am writing you about your mother.

Your mother is a blessing inside you. She made this house you left and entered so often a home. She sent you off with a tear, a cheer, a wave, a smile. She greeted you with love at the door when you ran all the way down the hill from school, when you were covered with mud from the valley, when you brought a friend for overnight, and when you came home later than we thought possible.

Your mother shed a tear and her voice broke when the evening news was too severe, when children were abused or abandoned. She went through the mail to see where we could give help to the world—at home or far away. Her sound decisions kept our family in the black. She made sure you had a gift for God on Sundays, and that you knew why you took an offering to church.

She made sure she heard where you hurt, and gave you medicine that healed and preventive advice before the next hurt. When a tragedy hit our family, she went into the night to face the pain, ease the hurt, stay until all were safe. While I stayed frozen with fear in bed, your mother braved the hurt with you. She faced many storms with the spirit and heart of a pioneer. She did not retreat if she saw an enemy. A mother tiger was no more fierce or caring.

Your mother filled our home with your music. You brought in cellos and pianos and violins and oboes and guitars. She took you to lessons and made dinners while you practiced within earshot. Her piano playing healed tense times and prevented others. She went to the piano when hearts needed quieting. Hymns old and new, and her own hymns bathed the rooms.

How pretty your rooms were. Your mother sewed your curtains, bedspreads, pillows. She combined colors and pictures that made your room like you. She wanted your rooms to look as nice as you, and she gave you habits you now practice without knowing.

Your mother talked about truth, fairness, diversity. She treated each of you the way she knew you, the way you were growing. You did not receive the same kind of toys or gifts or treatment. She knew your differences; she talked of them with you. She reminded you of your value, your purpose, your faith. She hugged you when you solved important matters. She fought you on issues that would destroy you. And she let you go when you had to find out for yourself. She cared about children's rights and about your rights. When you were treated unfairly—in ways that injured you, she stood up for you. She talked to your teachers as through they were your second parents. She made sure they knew you, and that she knew what they thought of you.

Your mother kept you in touch with our families. She saw to it that you knew our stories, and that you wrote thank-you notes when gifts came. She let you take turns talking long distance, and she read family letters aloud so you kept up with family history.

You were dressed well. Your mother dressed you in homemade clothes. Can you hear the sewing machine hum? Can you see her there finishing a beautiful dress for you to wear in a few hours? When you had needs, she looked at everything and decided how to meet each need. Her deadlines were often met to the second. You enjoyed spontaneity with your mother. Your many interests in nature, music, relationships were spawned and guided by her.

Your mother talked about God with you. She wanted you to know things of faith and value and beauty. She asked you questions, gave her opinions, spoke of her own faith. Sometimes she quoted Shakespeare to you instead of the Bible, but the meanings were close.

She made sure our table was beautiful, that candles burned. She saw that church-year festivals were celebrated, that you could play and pray the great stories of God. She cared about our prayer times together, and she has not relinquished this legacy of prayer. She prays for you when waking, when going to sleep. She prays each day for you and for many, many others. She knows when people hurt and when they mark anniversaries. Tiny drawings decorate her letters.

Your mother loves our two cats. She knows when other cats need catnip, and she sends it to them in homemade nap mats, which cats like. Your mother has helped you celebrate salamanders, turtles, white rats, boa constrictors, raccoons, chickens, rabbits, hamsters, owls. Your mother has hunted through bird and reptile books until you learned what you had found, what you were holding.

Both her names are in the Bible: Naomi, Lois. Strong women from Old and New Testament stories. Those namesakes are her mentors and models.

Before your mother and I married, we talked about our love for each other and our love for you. From the beginning, our conversation spoke of you—not yet conceived or born. That was forty-seven years ago. You are still part of the love we have. She gave you the life you enjoy so much.

If you want to bring your mother a flower she'll like, it best be one she can plant. She has a green thumb and a passion for gardens.

This is Mother's Day. What part of your mother will you feel and love inside yourself? What will you take into your years to come as her legacy to you?

Your mother tucked a blessing inside you. Believe me.

Love, Dad

My Father

My father would have told you of his homeland.

You did not know my father, except by hearsay. Five foot ten, one hundred fifty pounds, a tenor, a German immigrant teacher. He worked harvest fields of Kansas and Nebraska, taught country school, then went through college and seminary to become a minister at age thirty-four. His name was Heinrich Friedrich Ludwig Brokering. He bore names handed down through generations and a family name dating back to records written on pigskins in 1460. Father was an immigrant, a citizen of two countries. I believe he was always homesick.

I remember Father seated at an old Remington typewriter. With his own hunt-and-peck method, he typed long letters in two languages, which he read to our family before mailing. They were about the family, crops, current events, family curiosity, and they always ended with a mini-sermon and benediction. Father was a pastor to his siblings across the seas during the years of World War I, through the years of Hitler and World War II. He worried about us here, and he worried about his family in Germany whom he did not visit since 1907. Father died in 1952 at age sixty-nine.

Father's letters were cherished in the "old country," where they were read and studied. In 1948 many were given to me from the drawer of a chiffonier where they'd been stored. In the letters I read about the births and lives of my dad and Clara and their five children.

I often felt his homesick spirit. We loved when letters came from his European family and wanted the envelope lining that made overseas' letters doubly special.

Father was a farm boy who knew how to build a shed with old lumber and how to fix tires with a crowbar, sandpaper, glue, patch, and pump on a country road. Father fixed things. I remember his preacher salary being just enough so we weren't poor. We were busy saving money, so we mostly made things we needed, used old boards, mended, nailed things together one more time. Nothing was thrown away. Bailing wire was a blessing.

Father taught us things I do not remember ever learning. I don't know when I didn't know how to dig a garden, hoe, rake hay, milk a cow, build a tree house. We built a warm-brooder for chicks that came delivered in the mail and left in our mailbox with the red flag up. We were proud that our father—a preacher—could build, shock wheat, hand plow; that he knew how to stack hay in the barn so it would cure and not burn or mold from heat. Father taught us to live close to the earth, to know oak from cedar and walnut. He planted trees wherever we lived, and I carried many buckets of water to save those trees during hot drought seasons.

Father worried about health. He took steam baths in the kitchen, pouring water over hot rocks to get rid of bronchitis. He insisted we put skimmed cream on cold sores and chapped hands. Father had opinions about staying well that became family orders. We seldom had a doctor in; there was none nearby, and we saved money that way. Sometimes we were cured by long prayers at supper.

Father knew how to work with farmers. That is why when my youngest sister was born, we moved so father could become a country preacher. Like all country preachers, we had acres of land that we farmed, gardened, and kept as pasture. Dad made sure God's "Call" included a small barn. We kept chickens, a cow, sometimes goats. Father knew how to pick a good milk cow at a farm auction. There were five ways to tell a good cow, and I know them all. He knew how to help a cow when it gave birth, when it was bitten by a poisonous snake, when it was bloated from eating wet clover.

Dad helped people in the harvest field when rains and storms hurried over a farm. I think I always knew how to shock grain, drive horses, or talk with farmers. My brother and I rummaged through piles of scrap iron and made one bike out of the parts of ten. I did not know there were new bikes; I thought they were put together the way my father made chicken pens.

Mostly I remember Father studying his sermons, writing each word just right to please God. He walked the floor upstairs, saying a sermon over and over so he knew it almost by heart, and so his pronunciation sounded American.

Father was always in bilingual rural parishes. He wanted his congregations to know God's Word in English as well as German. I can hear him insist, "This is America; we must worship in English." He spoke German with those who were older and knew God in German. He believed children and young people should know God in English. This meant I had to memorize hymns, Bible verses, and Martin Luther's entire Small Catechism in German and English. I helped Father teach high-German to low-German-speaking country children whose parents wanted them to learn about God in German. With Father as our teacher, we children stood to recite verses or tell Bible stories. He never used the braided leather whip he inherited in the school desk, but we often felt the sting of not knowing. What we learned we sang in hymns, which father led with a loud tenor voice as he played the reed pump organ.

My father had a yearning, a kind of *Heimweh*—homesick spirit. He was an immigrant who missed his homeland. I believe that Mother, too, wanted to visit the homestead her father had told her about. Are we all somehow incomplete? Do we all have a yearning for places we will never go to see?

Father had more patience with others than with me. He taught others to play piano, organ, and violin. Father knew the mind of God, and gave me information about God, obedience to God, that I still need today. My mother taught me the heart of God.

I did many things with you that my father would have enjoyed doing with you.

Your Grandfather Brokering would have crossed his legs and given you a "horse ride" on his bouncing foot. He would have played you songs—with mistakes—and helped you ride a cow or goat. He would have showed you a pasture he knew by heart and lifted you upon the seat of machinery on some farm. He would have carried you on his shoulders to make you tall. You would have seen him close his eyes and pray for long times. Perhaps his voice would have broken when you left to go home, for inside his stern posture was a soft and homesick spirit.

Father died when I was twenty-six and he was sixty-nine. I wish I had asked more about his feelings, heard his reason for immigrating, his childhood stories, what it was like to see the Statue of Liberty, his time on Ellis Island. I wish he had told me stories about how he met my mother in a Minnesota garden while selling Bibles one summer, about his escape when the Ku Klux Klan chased him, about what it was like to be separated from his childhood family for fifty years. I wish I had written a song to sing just with him, thanked him for what he helped me learn and believe, and traveled with him to his homestead once.

I believe my many journeys around the world are living out your grandfather's homesick heart. Perhaps you, too, have learned to love travel because your grandfather never could. You are fulfilling his hope. So it is with a legacy.

Keep visiting your homestead.

Love, Dad

Have fun along the way.

I liked watching you wake up in the morning. I could hardly wait
to see you eat your favorite breakfast, which changed with the season.
We made pancakes to look like animals and faces and flowers.
We shaped French toast into art forms. We lit candles for joy.
Do you still light candles when you eat or when you talk together or when
you believe something special is happening in the world?

Create Worlds of Words

A word is a world.

When I was nineteen I had a teacher in a course called "Form Criticism." The course was about words, how each goes through times and communities that give the word its special meaning. Some words now in the dictionary were not there a few years ago. Words are powerful: they grow, they carry meanings that cause people to believe, wage battle, make love, debate, take sides, form covenants.

This professor showed me how a world is a universe, a swirling of feelings and thoughts, a collage of colors, a matrix of moving parts. He did for me what I hope I sometimes showed you, as we played at the table with photographs taken by Sister Noemi from St. Scholastica. We looked at a picture. We asked: "What do you see? What else? What else?" Sometimes I asked and your words and thoughts swirled like a whirlwind. Sometimes we wrote them down. I could not write as fast as you laughed your words. It was a glad time, for everything we saw and said was right.

Words are spaces inside with which we meet, play, dance, collaborate, covenant, disagree, and send messages. A good word is indeed a big world.

One of Sister Noemi's photos was an open dandelion, fuzz and seed ready to fly. Then came your words: "Blooming! Ripe! Ferris wheel! Merry-go-round! Circle! Lollipop! Ball! Balloon! Fourth of July! Cheering!" We were never finished. Words turned into sentences, and sentences into stories. So it is with the miracle of our own words.

The professor taught me that is how it is with words. He was a professor of theology, and the words he expanded were holy words. So also the words around our family table were special; the images with which we played felt holy. They were sacred for they were the words and sights and emotions you imaged. You, children of the Creator, did what God does: communicate. You exploded worlds of words. You created meaning, relationships, connections, and you laughed as you did so.

The professor was then called a liberal. I did not know what liberal meant. I think it must have meant he *liberated,* because he went outside the dots—but never forgot the center. The center is the point from which we draw a circumference with a compass. It all reminds me of the rules about piano notes and piano playing that you learned; then you bent the rules for improvisation. The professor helped me bend rules without breaking them. How freeing that can be.

You each have a way to enjoy words. Your words whirl, dance, explore, fly, ponder. You have taken more from my words than I gave you. Your words are so great and many now that I sometimes need Webster to follow you. There comes a time when a word outgrows its time and moves into a next generation.

Keep growing your words, your worlds. And keep me posted so we are in the same world.

Love, Dad

Stand Up for Honor

When I was little, we children always stood when the Heckels came into the room.

They were older, and we learned that standing was a sign of honor. As I recall, part of the reason for standing was the puzzles Mr. Heckel brought as gifts and the cookies Mrs. Heckel baked for us. Honor was a two-way street.

Honor your father and your mother. I memorized that commandment in German and English, and all the Bible verses that seemed to support it. In my old Memory Book, some verses were marked with one cross and others with two. The double-crossed verses were supposed to be required memory work. But somehow my father had me learn them all, crosses or no crosses. I did not always feel honored by this assignment.

What I liked best among all the verses was one Bible sentence that said, "Fathers, provoke not your children to anger." That made it a two-way street for me. Honor to Mother and Father was something we also felt coming from them. Honor was a loop, a circle.

How did I honor you?

I remember asking you about your day at school, wanting to see what you were inventing in the garage workshop, asking to see knots you'd learned to tie in scouts, and taking photos of your scout work. I remember going with you to look for animal tracks in mud, for beauty to photograph in winter, for ways to build a better dog house for Scamper. Honor was something I felt when I was with you. It happened when we did things together.

I feel your honor when you mention my friends of long ago to your colleagues. I feel honor when you take me to rivers in Tokyo where you walk to look at birds that thrill you, that remind you of birds in our Minnesota valley. I am honored when you show your friends a book I wrote, or want to take home cookies your mother baked at Christmas. You honor me when you call me Dad or Father. And I feel honored when you sometimes call me Herb; it is the name of a friend, and I am honored to be your friend as well as your father. I feel honored when you recite your new lyrics and want ideas for one more line in a poem that is stuck. It's an honor when you phone and ask, "How are you?" And it's a very great honor to hear you close our conversation with "I love you."

Honor means to exalt, lift up, revere. It is a tribute we give God, which causes us to rise or bow, raise our hands and be silent. I have seen you stop to touch a tree we planted when you were little. That's honor. I have heard you tell of something we allowed you to do that was special, daring, beautiful when you were little. That's honor. I have seen you run to hug me in an airport, and hold me the way I held you when you were little. That's honor. I have seen you be silent before a meal, sometimes whispering a prayer, sometimes sitting in quiet reverence. That is honor.

Honor is not automatic. When there was anger in my child heart it was hard to honor my father. Mother warmed the feelings, and soon the honoring spirit returned. The commandment says that honoring father and mother and children will make our years long. I believe that. It may not mean that we get to be older, but that our days and years are fuller and richer and seem longer.

Just to stand when older people enter the room is not real honor; the outer form needs an inner spirit. The cookies and the puzzles that Heckels brought, and knowing that they knew our names and loved our parents dearly—that is why I liked standing when they came in the room.

Honoring is a graceful way to live together.

Love, Dad

Go for the Green

Earth is growing green again.

The long winter is warming. A brown and grey earth turns into spans and horizons of green. Everywhere I look this April, it's green, green, green.

It is easy for me to see the green and the bloom in you and in myself. We are created to be green.

Spring fever is green; it's a newness inside, a wanting out again and again. The child's soul breaks through my body and wants to run and fly and play, just as seeds and birds are doing all around. We have been given this green season. At seventy I feel it more than ever.

There is so much new to do. We have so much potential. We can begin new work. We can have more than one profession, more than one career. You do. I encouraged you to take a double major, at least several minors, in college. Most professions can be honorable and fulfilling. When you waited tables, I was proud of your style. When you repair houses, I brag of your gifts to make an old room new. When you directed theater, I wanted to take bows with you and catch the bouquets. When you stir dreams of youth in your neighborhood and gather them to hear each others' dreams —and do this without pay—I am proud. Some mornings I wake and think myself a waiter. I feel the newness of this new work. And I want to learn guitar and piano, to swim, draw, fly kites. Today I feel springtime green.

I feel new poems in me, new stories, new connections of metaphors, new images, new gifts. I want to paint on easels, play Max Reger on the organ, create guitar music, write new lyrics. I want to record a country and western hit in Nashville.

Be glad for new feelings, new work, new kinds of thoughts. Do not give in to a dead-end life.

You invent. I can tell your excitement on the phone when you take a new step. This week you flew to talk with a friend, a financial backer. You both agreed: "Let's go for it." What is "it"? It is new life. Go for the green.

Green time always comes with its own patterns. The robin eggs outside our door have hatched, the young birds already have grown and flown. All this in fourteen days. Four eggs were laid, four robins flew in four consecutive days. How organized creation is.

We have new possibilities in us, and they wait to be fulfilled in order, in beauty, in wonder. I looked into the last baby robin's eyes and said, "Have a wonderful flight." With baby robin staring in my eyes, I said, "I love you." In an hour it had flown. I have a new friend in the sky. In October it will join one billion robins in the flyways.

We all have new ways to live, to fly. I love you. Have a good flight.

It's spring and I see maple leaves unfolded. It happened overnight with springtime showers. We can no longer see the valley through the mesh of a million small green leaves. There are layers and layers of green hues before us. You know the green here in the valley. You know the springtime green inside yourself.

Green replaces death in us. Old cells want to be new. Old thoughts can be reshaped, made fresh. Feelings find their deep wells again. Spirits fly. One billion robins came up the Mississippi flyway. A million baby robins joined them. All creation is going green, flying.

I, too, am green. That is why I write new stories, new prayers, new lyrics. I look into these new words to you, and I see myself a seed in spring, whispering to those who will live after me. I will live on in this greenness.

Love, Dad

Play Peek-a-boo

When you were little you liked to play peek-a-boo.

You liked seeing and not seeing. You liked appearing and dis-appearing. We hid around corners, under towels, behind tables. Now you see us, now you don't: magic! A lot of life was that way, a kind of magic. The game of revealing and concealing is old in you.

One day we went to a magic shop. You learned how to make things disappear, reappear. Your best friends sat in the front row of your backyard magic show and tried to see through the mystery. I still feel that excitement in me, trying to figure out a revelation right under my eyes.

Sometimes play peek-a-boo again.

Peek-a-boo magic is the mystery of revelation, expecting the impossible, dreaming, seeing through a maze, being amazed. We need the gift of such magic in our lives. Practice the joy of peek-a-boo. Look at one thing, watch, watch closely, see through it. Look away, then look back. Look at a tiny seed slowly and carefully. Look away, then look back. See the stem, the bloom, the tree, the fruit, the new seed. Slowly see the cycle. Look at the snow, the dormant sleep. Shut your eyes, look again. See the spring, the new life.

Look at a person near you. Look carefully. Look away. Then look back, slowly, to when that person was younger. See that person as a year younger, many years younger, a child, a toddler, a baby, just born. Slowly know what a parent feels as a child grows, unfolds, appears again and again through the years.

Play peek-a-boo through all your years.

This week a woman I didn't recognize reminded me that I taught her to peek through a hole in a small piece of birch bark. That was thirty years ago. She still looks at life this way, to focus, penetrate, when too much is going on. She remembered peeking from childhood.

60

I remember when you were little, we placed our fingers over your eyes so you could not see, then see, not see, see. Why did you laugh so? What made you so happy with the game? Was it the not seeing, then seeing? Do you like it today when you can't see and then you can? Does peek-a-boo make you laugh today?

There is a word I liked hearing in seminary lectures: "revelation." Revelation contains this mystery of expecting the impossible; of not seeing then seeing; of receiving a vision; dreaming of a new Jerusalem, a new world; picturing a life to come. God's game of peek-a-boo.

Sometimes you placed our fingers over your eyes when you wanted to play peek-a-boo. We never held our hands over your eyes more than a few seconds. That was long enough for the darkness.

In the book of Revelation, the writer John sketches pictures of hope and light, of a new heaven and a new earth, a city of God with golden streets and wondrous gates. His is a revelation of salvation. It's there, it's real; it's just hidden in darkness. God will take our hands off our eyes. The great peek-a-boo.

Keep playing.

Love, Dad

Take Time

I like timepieces—clocks, watches, sundials, metronomes.

We have three clocks in the house. Sometimes all three strike at once. I like that. You gave me a Storm watch. People admire the watch; you said they would.

In the night I often look out the window and guess the time. I have learned to tell time by shadows—moon shadows at night, sun shadows by day. When the Iron Curtain fell, I bought seven watches in East Germany, the land of Bach. The first watch I wound when a Bach concert began. The others are waiting for their first beat of time.

Why is time so much in my thinking? Is it because in the middle of a Christmas season my brother fell to his death, and Christmas felt like a funeral, like Good Friday? Did I then begin to know that all kinds of time coincide, that times intersect? Time is not just a long, straight line. Time has layers, intersections, overlays. Time bunches up, jams. Time is more than clocks and calendars on a wall.

I like time because it gives us all kinds of times: springtime, summertime, nighttimes, mornings and breakfast times, birthday times. We tell times by their temperature, the color of the grass, the height of the sun, the sound of birds, the stage of blossoms. Nature tells us times. Time also has to do with moods: joyful, sad, tender, critical times. I have *felt* times.

Time and times have woven the fabric of our life together. When you were little, you knew when it was time for napping, eating, crying, stretching. Time was written in your body. There came the time to crawl, to sit, walk, run. Your small and large muscles told you which times you loved and which you didn't. Your brain waves kept time. In due time, you learned to read, do math, memorize plays, play instruments. You sang the song from

Ecclesiastes, "For everything there is a time." You helped me write a book, *In Due Season*.

Sometimes we rushed time in spring, planting hibiscus and pansies too early, and in a late frost they died. Summertime came fast, and it was too late to plant the apple tree. Time is fixed inside seed. We read seed packages and obeyed their instructions about time.

Remember how it felt to come home when the sun was low in the sky? We knew it took twelve days for robin eggs to hatch. The big elm bloomed at the end of April. Full moon in springtime was around the 28th of the month. When squirrels buried acorns, we knew it was time to put on storm doors. Mother nature was our timekeeper.

Time gave you expectation, the gift of hope. How you practiced waiting before Christmas. You opened one present a week, during Advent, to make waiting time bearable. Time is what makes a circus exciting. You watched the timing of acrobats, and we gasped and held our breath. Timing is what made some pieces so beautiful in band and orchestra. When you got the timing just right, your rock band sounded great, and you knew it.

Time comes in tiny bits and pieces scattered through a world of days and years. Keep learning to tell time in all its wonderful forms. Make time your gift.

Love, Dad

Look Down, Look Up

Climb a tree again.

I can no longer climb the elm tree in the yard of my childhood
Nebraska home. I loved the top of that tree sixty years ago. From
there I could look over the walnut trees on our seven acres of land
and see the Tuxhorn farm. I could spot the tin-can holes and tiny
greens around them that made up my homemade golf course.
From the top of that elm I could see the roof of our white country
church, the creek running past the Knipplemeyer farm; I could
look out over the high hedgerow to the horizon in the east. Below
me was our house and the cellar door on which I liked snuggling
with my dog in the sun, saying nothing, getting faithful looks and
friendly licks. The top of that elm was a special place.

Climb a tree somewhere and see what you saw from the
sycamore in our San Antonio yard. Perspective is a wondrous gift
we have. Everything looks different from a high place.

The tower of my father's Nebraska church was another height
I liked. From there I could see, close-up, the giant steel bell
inscribed with a Bible verse. I could see the heavy rope that rang
the bell for worship and the smaller rope tied to a clapper for
tolling when someone died. I can still feel the height of the church
tower as I watched a funeral procession slowly appear over the hill.
That is when the tolling of bells began. Often rain and mud
moved the procession slowly. The tolling time doubled; so did my
feelings for the people in the cars — men wearing black armbands,
women wearing black veils.

From the church tower I could also look east to the Norbrook
farm, and if the wind was right, I could hear the braying of the Norbrook donkey that fathered the mules in our countryside. I liked
that sound. And I liked Virgil Norbrook, who seldom shaved, didn't
come to church, and wasn't married. He made the highest bids on

pies sold at our annual school play and pie auction. From the tower I could see the Greenfield School, where Virgil Norbrook later lived, and which he kept just as it had always been: no electric lights, no telephone, no running water—a museum. A museum is what I saw from the tower sixty years ago. A museum is what I can still see as I look down from the church tower all these years later.

What are the high places you've climbed to look at everything in a closer or more distant way, to let feelings run over you like wind? Hold on tight so you're safe and can look far.

Where do we find new perspectives to keep our views from growing static? Perspectives don't always have to come from climbing high places. Once I was caught in a culvert; I could not crawl through and had to back out. When you're retreating from something and you can't see behind you, you get another kind of perspective. I discovered this; I am sure you've done the same. Lots of times you have to go backwards without looking. And you discover a new way to look at things.

When you were growing up, you told of climbing to the top of a water tower and using a super-eight camera to take pictures looking straight down. You were where birds fly, you looked with a real bird's-eye view, and you felt safe. Do you still go high?

You also went into an old copper mine and dropped rocks into deep, dark shafts to hear the echo many seconds later. The dark silence, the waiting, and somehow feeling safe in that dark waiting is now part of you. You have enriched yourself for perspectives that can see into places silent, dark, and deep—places that need waiting.

How filled we are with high and low places, with ways we measure our lives, relationships, conversations.

Stay in touch with places where you looked at your world from a distance or close up or through. Perspective is what keeps God's world from being flat, too even, only a globe.

Love, Dad

Enjoy Yourself

What makes you glad?

What did I do when you were little that made you smile, feel glad—that still thrills your spirit?

I liked riding on my father's shoulders and being higher than he was. I liked holding on to his hair and feeling I was riding horseback. Touching the hair of a loved one, running my fingers over their face, being close to them, still makes me glad.

Remember when you'd hold me like I was a child? When done in a right spirit it was joyful. You were someone you'd be someday—grown up, an adult. I was someone I was before—a baby. This joy of pretending showed in pageants when you were angels with a white robe and a circle of stars over your head.

It's fun to be more than we are.

You laughed on Halloween. Masks and costumes transformed you into characters, animals, celebrities for a night. Inside you were more than ordinary feelings. You walked up streets like TV sets, monkeys, lions that growled and never hurt, someone in *Star Wars*, a pumpkin.

Pretending is still joyful.

You liked waiting for a present to be opened if the waiting was not too long. (Waiting time has limits.) Waiting is for guessing, hoping, expecting, believing. Not yet knowing but believing is a virtue.

Waiting can be fun.

A door in the brain opens when we laugh, praise, rejoice, share a gift. It sends out healing messages and medicine. You liked watching someone unwrap a gift you had given. You watched their eyes more than the gift. I watched your faces when you opened gifts from your mother and me. That was the main gift, your amazement. We still surprise each other.

Our family loved fun. We liked contrasts, surprises, serendipity, noticing more than meets the eye, seeing new connections, turning thoughts into a song. We liked finding out what made a homemade go-cart run faster. We liked welding together pieces of metal to see what they might become and be named. We made more than the most of things.

I was glad when mother rubbed my chest with camphor, placed a soft towel on my chest, pulled the flannel quilt to my chin, kissed me, and said I'd be well soon. I liked rubbing her neck when she had migraine headaches, hearing her hum what sounded like *Amen, Amen,* until she was better. She made me feel better in that same twenty minutes. I didn't laugh, but I was glad.

What makes you glad? I liked going to a circus with you, watching people in midair fall in love and cling to each other. Lying on our backs on hillsides, we saw chariots in white clouds. We wrote notes on balloons at funerals and sent messages of hope into the skies. We pinned words on kite tails and sent joy into the clouds. We gave pets special burials and smiled when the tears were gone.

I liked your waking in the morning. I could hardly wait to see you eat your favorite food, which changed with the seasons. We made pancakes shaped like animals and faces and flowers. We shaped French toast into art forms. We lit candles and ate in good moods. That was a joy. Do you still light candles when you eat or when you talk quietly or when you believe something special is happening in the world?

I liked it when you waved good-bye to go into your school world. Sometimes you waved when we could no longer see you. Can you remember your words when you came into the front door with something you wrote or painted at school? Can you remember a good friend you brought home to stay overnight? Do you still thrill with a close friend, being near and knowing something together that you don't even need to talk about?

I was glad when we held hands and said a prayer before eating something that looked very special. If the prayer was too long, it was not so joyful. When I was little, I liked a prayer four words long: "Abba, dear Father. Amen." I also liked singing bedtime prayers aloud and fast, finishing before my siblings. I did not like it when I had to pray them again slowly, with careful thought. I liked being happy when going to sleep. You often giggled yourselves to sleep.

Is bedtime still a glad time?

I will never know all that makes you glad. I do know that our joy is a healing power. I wish you joy and gladness.

Love, Dad

I know the feeling.

Sometimes we are sorry—truly sorry—and wanting forgiveness much later.
That is how it sometimes was with our family. We requested and received
love late. Love is not always there on time. But love can be retroactive.
It was sometimes so for me. Is it so for you?
The pendulum on our living room clock swings back and forth,
going backwards to go ahead, it seems.

Family Forgiveness

It is not good to sleep with anger inside the soul.

Anger will make us tired. It will live inside and sleep deeply there until it is somehow cast out. Love is stronger than anger; love can cast out anger.

I do not remember that we ever slept before kissing and making up when there was anger in the house. But it may be that the kissing was not enough, and not everything was forgiven. Sometimes, maybe, with me the kiss-and-make-up ritual masked real feelings, things that needed to be said and done. Somehow, using religious words and pious phrases made everything seem right to me. But there must have been times when you thought the words too hollow, the hugs meaningless motions. You did not say so or cry out because your hurt was too painful, your anger still alive and hidden within.

Sometimes we are sorry—truly sorry—and wanting forgiveness much later. That is how it sometimes was with our family. We requested and received love late. Love is not always there on time. But love can be retroactive. It was sometimes so for me. Is it so for you? The pendulum on our living room clock swings back and forth, going backwards to go ahead, it seems.

Time swings, circles, retrieves, and loops back on itself. Sometimes forgiveness is that way. Sometimes it comes on the third or the fifth sunset, or later. Forgiveness may need to go back into the past.

Do you think of these things?

I have forgiven you as completely as I am able. Sometimes my love came slow. If there were times I forgave late, when the sun was low in our Minnesota valley, it was still high in the west. I borrowed the sun in California while you were already asleep in Minnesota. We can do that.

We live on a timeline where forgiveness is not instant, where sunsets roll slowly westward over a series of horizons—sunset after sunset. Sunsets and forgiving are continuous. They are always there, always happening.

Sometimes I have forgiven you by moonlight. I have kissed you when stars were waking. I felt our love in the face of your sleep, and in the joy of your waking, and in the way we ate cereal at the morning table.

When the sun was rising I knew forgiveness had wakened and our love had lived through the night.

Did I tell you how I felt about forgiveness as the sun went down? Did you feel our new love when the same sun rose? Sunrise makes a circle with sunset, forgiveness makes a circle with love.

So I say a new saying: Feel love before your sun goes down, and feel love again at dawn.

Love, Dad

Compassion for Peace

Sometimes feel the evening news.

Let your heart touch your mind as you watch reports of what's happening here and abroad. If you feel callused, either turn the news off or look at it with a deeper eye. Have compassion for a world that will always have poverty, pain, and weapons.

Keep your eyes on children with bloated bellies, with flies drinking their tired watery eyes, with broad smiles when they are handed a cup of soup. Keep your compassion busy.

When I was barely twenty, I had not seen much grand-scale pain. World War II was ended but not over. I walked and drove through streets of Hamburg, Bremen, Frankfurt, and other burned and bombed cities. I saw women gathering and piling bricks to rebuild what was still broken and warm from war. I felt their eyes filled with pain and pride at once. Gangs ran the streets looking for bread, bribing for drink. Did I tell you enough about those years? Did I share my passion for peace and my hope for the oppressed? Did I talk with you about people in want? Were my stories as vivid as *The Three Bears*, *The Velveteen Rabbit*, and *The Billy Goats' Gruff*? Did you learn to hate war, to love peace, to care about people who suffer? Did we work to build a better world when you were children?

I did not write my congressman or march for peace. I did lead thousands on pilgrimages through the Iron Curtain, where we visited holocaust survivors and heard their stories, carried candles, sang "Blowin' in the Wind." You helped me pack for those pilgrimages, and you waited for me to return home, thankful for this nation and this home, glad to make pancakes for breakfast, wash you in deep suds, sing about the Muffin Man, say home-made prayers with you.

What do you do when news is too hard to see? I remember that sometimes you cried when you looked. You had nightmares, and you stayed awake looking for bombs that never landed on our city. Later, you drove to Madison to carry banners. You have boycotted people you felt were poor role models for children.

You have not told me of all your passion or compassion. I have seen some of it in your tears, your face, your tone of voice. I have heard it in the peace songs you memorized and played in rock groups. I have felt your caring in stories you told immigrant children on your street, in time capsules you helped them make and bury for children in the twenty-first century. I heard your passion as you rehearsed a holocaust symphony in a Tokyo orchestra. I sensed compassion in a book you sent me to read. I felt it at my bedside when you watched me heal.

How did our family share compassion? How much did we know about each other's peaceful spirit? How did we learn about human rights at home? What did we say when prejudice and stories of enemies entered our conversation? How did we receive persons of color into the family?

Thirty years ago we began making annual cross-country drives to a retreat center in the Cascades. Year after year it was our family peace pilgrimage. The way you laughed and played in back of the station wagon, singing, sharing, pretending, mending wounded trolls, and sewing eyes back into teddy bears is still clear to me.

Let your mind touch your heart, and let your emotions tend your mind. It requires the whole person to make peace.

Love, Dad

Fear of Fathers

Fear finds its hiding place.

Have I frightened you and we have not spoken about the fear? Have I angered you and it lies lurking deep in you? Tell me soon.

My father was a good man. He taught me about God with all his heart. Yet he frightened me, and the fright stayed shut inside me for many years. The fear lived in me and grew.

On parish visits, my father laughed and smiled a lot, and he told stories at weddings. He laughed hardest when Mr. Hoefling told jokes he'd read in a farmer's magazine. He helped farmers with their harvest when rain clouds blew in from the northwest. Father taught me the mind of God, he helped me learn by heart good psalms and scripture verses. He helped me study God's love and grace and faith and taught me healing stories. I think of Father often every day.

But in my early life, he frightened me; and the fear stayed with me.

Father studied many hours to write well and to say well what he would preach. While we were playing downstairs, I heard his feet stomping on the upstairs floor in our country parsonage. Then we stopped laughing and playing. We grew quiet. We colored and drew pictures with mother. Or we went outside to play. I memorized the words, "*Sei Still*. Be quiet."

Something little grew inside me, something that frightened. I feared my father, and I began to fear my heavenly Father, too. I couldn't believe the Bible verses enough.

Have I hid in you any fearful feelings? Tell me while we are together, while we can still talk about the feelings.

I talked about these things with my doctor and cleared my soul of this childhood fear. This was thirty years after Father died. He would have listened to me, he would have talked with me; but I did not know how to begin the conversation. He would have confessed a homesickness for his homeland six thousand miles away by ship. He would have hugged me and told me stories about his father and dearest mother, but I did not ask him. I was busy playing, hoeing weeds, shocking wheat for farmers, going to high school, and then hiking to college. We would have kissed to make up, but I did not reach out. My mother did the kissing in our home.

There comes an age and a time when we are on our own, and we can no longer place responsibility with a parent. There comes a time to forgive, be reconciled, and move on with life. I waited very long for that time. Do not wait so long with me. I will talk with you about fears I may have caused you. Do this while I am with you.

My father helped us sing almost every sentence we believed about God. He pumped a little reed organ in a white country school, and we sang our faith. In the midst of music I still feared God too much, and sometimes my father. Now I know it wasn't only my father's fear in me. There was a world war. There was anger and hatred in the neighborhood. I wore a body brace to school, and some classmates called me "Hunch Back of Notre Dame." My father befriended me, bought me a body brace he could not afford. He sent us all to college when he did not have the money. He helped us pronounce words correctly while he paced the floor improving his own immigrant accent. He showed us how to build the best tree houses, and how to choose a good cow at a country auction. He made prayer at night and when we woke a healing habit.

Fathers play tag with fathers. What have I placed inside you, for good or evil? My father and I could have settled things all in one hour, maybe in a minute. Talk to me.

Love, Dad

Sorrow and Hope

We mourn, then we go on.

How will it be when one of your siblings dies? What will you say, think, feel? What will you do?

When I was nine years old, my brother Paul fell from a willow in the winter, onto a frozen creek. He died two days after Christmas. I had one gift from him still to unwrap. I remember that Sunday as though it were yesterday. I believe all the nine years before that Sunday—and some thereafter—merged into three days of December 1935.

I was young, and I was sad. I was nine. On Monday I split wood. We tolled the church bell eighteen times to tell the countryside the news of a young death. The farmers of the parish cried in our house. Our little family went into the kitchen corner and ate warm milk poured over pieces of toast with salt and pepper. Father prayed a prayer from the Bible which I did not understand: "The Lord has given, the Lord has taken; blessed be the name of the Lord. Amen." I can still smell the flowers in the northeast parlor, the room which we saved in winter for special occasions like this.

I carried this story in me like a giant toy. It was too large; I did not know how to hold it. In a dream I met Paul in a favorite hideaway, the hayloft. He told me he was in heaven and everything was fine. I told my family the dream. I promised God every night in a prayer that I'd be a missionary like Paul had wished to be. But I prayed: "Please send me to Africa instead of New Guinea, God, if you want to."

What did I give you from this deep experience of mine? I gave you something of my childhood fears of death, I know. I also gave you good lyrics and hymns about willows and wind and water and winter and resurrection. You felt my loneliness and my silence, my worries about my own illnesses and yours. You felt my fear of sickness and dying. I also gave you stories of springtime and pictures of Easter time. We raised chicks in the spring and planted flowers as my own signs of life after death. I was in six ambulances fearing death, and I recovered with the love of nurses, doctors, and family. This all happened while we were a young family.

You did not want this fear of death inside you, and you said so. You helped me write stories and poems about hope and winter turning to spring and God healing the sick and raising the dead. You kept your sights on springtime.

What do you believe about hope now? How do friends around you talk about death and life?

Death and resurrection, fear and hope, Good Friday and Easter have always been real in our home. We have nurtured dying plants until they were well. You have buried wings and remnants of animals in gardens and showered them with love and prayers. You have shared a hurt that was deep inside me, that needed years to open to heal.

Lyrics of your songs, too, speak of death and life. You sit with friends during funerals. You know what balances, what bends, what breaks. You have let me hold you when I could not be alone with my fears. We planted gardens on Slovak mountainsides as memorials to hope amid death. We have photographed seasons of sleep and rising.

Uncle Clar is almost ninety-seven. Soon there'll be another rally of his siblings. As his siblings reach their mid-nineties, they cheer each other toward heaven. Each meeting time is a grand party, on earth and in heaven.

What will you do when a sibling dies?

I believe you will do what you have already done: cry, be angry, be silent, believe, write a poem, sing a song, smile, make a toast, tell stories, touch each other, and live on.

Love, Dad

Part of You

Where are you now?

How close are we? Not in miles, but in all other ways. How close are we?

When each of you was born I could see something of myself in you. Yet you were from an ancient pool of genes. You had eyes and a nose and a chin inherited from others in our genealogy. You were not only a reproduction of mother and father. Where did that gift for math come from, and your perfect pitch, your marvelous moods? From where came the tiny differences you carry as inheritance?

Through the years I saw more and more of myself in you, sometimes less and less. Now I see more and more of you in me.

You may recall my weekend on a mountain outside Los Angeles years ago. I led a youth retreat with two hundred junior high students on the topic, "The Nicene Creed." Did they want to study The Nicene Creed for three days on a beautiful mountain, I asked them.

No.

So I told them a story about a worldwide church assembly in the year A. D. 325, in the city of Nicea. Bishops and clergy came on camels, horses, and by foot from all parts of earth to a special convention. The purpose was to decide: "How is Jesus connected to God? Is Jesus divine?" In the story of that Nicean assembly, I told them of delegates looking for one word—one word—for a secretary to write into the minutes. The word needed to be a preposition about the connection between Jesus and God.

Prepositions. It took time for the youth to get into this idea. They rehearsed their knowledge of a dozen prepositions: *for, in, with, from, around…* We studied each as a spatial word. How close is *with*? How close is *from*? Is Jesus *in* God? Is Jesus *for* God? Prepositions were in the air everywhere. The morning went well.

Mealtimes at retreats have their own agenda. Food, laughter, meeting new girls and boys. Then came the afternoon. The topic would not be "The Nicene Creed." That they had agreed. Instead, there would be a hunt for the right preposition. They liked the Nicea story, but they still needed to find the one word the Nicean secretary would write to describe the connection between Jesus and God. One preposition.

At last, two hundred young people were ready to vote on the big preposition chosen in the year A.D. 325. The final two contending prepositions were written on the board: *with* and *of*. A boy made a speech in favor of "Jesus is *with* God." A girl made a short speech about "Jesus is *of* God." She said it was like being *of* your father and mother and yet being your own person. A quiet came over the two hundred. The vote was unanimous: *Of.* Jesus is of God.

The next days there were "of" banners and parades and "of" plays and games. There were "of" songs and stories. The word "of" flew on balloons, was painted on faces and tee shirts

When you were being formed, and when you were born, I felt you being "of" your father and mother. Very soon I noticed you were also "of" ancestors we never knew. As you grew, you also were "of" baby-sitters and relatives who held you, leaned over you, made you laugh, rocked you, loved you. You were "of" grandparents who prayed for you, sent you cards and gifts, told you stories. You were also "of" the children who played with you, the classmates and teachers in your kindergarten, grade school, high school, college. You were "of" Howdy Dowdy, Mr. Green Jeans, Abraham, Ruth, Jesus, and Mary.

Prepositions fascinate me. Each is about space, time. Each says how your body moves, tells where you are.

Are we of each other? We are also *with, for, against, from, through, into, around, behind* each other. Many mornings I walk with open arms toward you. You are thousands of miles away, city blocks away. I walk east, west, north, south. I embrace you with prepositions. My arms are around you; they reach from where I am across the miles into your home, your life.

The Nicene Creed still reads that Jesus is "*of* one substance with the Father."

Today I feel we are "of" each other and "of" God. I feel very close to you.

Love, Dad

Lasting Memories

I believe the past comes to life in my future.

When I was a child, I watched a wheat field pounded by a hail storm. Farmers raised their hats, then held them to their chests as they stood by, seeing their crops destroyed. It was also what farmers did when country funeral cars passed their fields. They stood in awe and honor. Death, either of a neighboring hired hand or of a field of grain, was something encountered with awe. Farm families were silent each time hail came. In September they sowed winter wheat again.

So it was when I was little. I still feel country silence after a storm, after death.

At any time the calf would be born. Our father always knew; he learned about such things when he was little in Europe. I went on tiptoe to the barn, peeking through a crack, listening for the breathing of the cow. While waiting, we spread clean straw to bed the mother and the newborn. The eyes of Bessie, the only cow we had, seemed knowing as we hung our kerosene lantern on a high nail. She lay in straw with wide open eyes. Sometimes tears ran. Deep inside her, God scripted a huge event. Bessie felt it coming, knew it. We watched her eyes for the miracle she would bring.

So it was when I was little. I still watch eyes for miracles.

My mother was often very quiet, in a world we could not enter. I wanted to see and feel what she saw and felt. All my life I was close to her, and each day she was someone new. We never tired of Mother; she was a treasure box of surprises and delight for us. Once I saw her smile so deeply I thought she would laugh aloud. No one else was there, and she did not notice me. What did my mother see that pleased her so?

So it was when I was little. Today, like Mother, I grow quiet with deep feelings and smiles, and others do not know my secret world.

We planted trees everywhere we lived. Small towns knew us by the trees we left behind. How often I held a sapling tree while my brother filled the planting hole with earth. We leaned the tree a trifle away from the sun. Soon enough the sun would draw the tree toward it. A tree had to be straight from all directions; it always grew a little toward the sun. That's how we planted every maple, apple, willow, and Dutch elm.

So it was when I was little. Still today, when you want something to grow straight, you need to consider it from all directions.

Every April, a baby robin was blown from a nest near my childhood home. We warned robins when they built their nests, for they did not know the winds across Nebraska. Mother was best at saving the babies that fell. She held them with a cotton cloth and never fingerprinted them. She did not steal the robin scent. How softly she fed them; they never heard her voice. She did not steal the song of mother robin from them. Together we put them back in their nests.

So it was when I was little. It is still the kindest compassion that honors the true nature of those we help.

Springtime willows in bloom were like furry kittens. Butterfly wings were soft as a spring breeze; we were careful never to pinch the wings. Baby rabbit fur made my fingers nuzzle. Summer thistles made my fingertips slow and careful. My fingertips were gentle when they rubbed October flannel. Woolly sheep made my fingers glad. Winter icicles made my fingers quick. Warm dishwater in cold December made my fingers pucker.

So it was when I was little. I can still feel all seasons in my fingertips.

Violets grew everywhere in the grass outside our Nebraska parsonage. The purple between green blades looked like tiny bouquets in a giant floral shop. How many tiny gifts I picked and brought to ones I loved. I never wrapped them in plastic or tied them with long ribbons. I held them tightly in my right hand and gave them into another hand. And when the hand took them from me, I watched the face. I did not just hear what they said. I remember how the faces looked when I gave them my violets.

So it was when I was little. Today, too, I notice eyes and faces when people take my bouquets of flowers or words.

You have touched butterflies and violets. Can you still feel their touch? Do your memories lead your feelings today?

Our past will guide us into the future.

Love, Dad

Heartbeats

When did you last make a valentine?

It's Valentine's Day, a day for hearts, reds and whites, lace, love, candy. When I was nine and ten, Valentine's Day was one of my favorite holidays. Never was red paper so pretty, and never was I more careful with scissors. I folded paper gently so the crease could be pressed out and not show. Mine would be like a valentine heart bought in the five-and-ten-cent store.

If the heart looked full and fat, I liked it. It had more love inside. I knew who would get the heart. If the heart turned out long and skinny, it would go to someone else. If it was crooked, I knew it was for Melvin because he liked me anyway.

Behind all the hearts I cut out was a lover I never quite knew. Giving away hearts was somehow mysterious, secretive. Putting valentines into a decorated box so it all seemed private helped. Making valentine hearts and giving them to each other was intimate. At age nine I did not know what to do with the intimacy I felt inside. Sometimes not putting my name on the heart at all, giving it to someone anonymously, felt best.

I still have a valentine you gave me forty years ago. That will not surprise you. I think I have some from seventy years ago.

I liked making a heart pattern out of newspaper, tracing around the pattern onto pink paper, cutting it out, pasting it down. This made a more perfect heart—no crease down the center. We layered the hearts from large to small, and mixed paper colors to put more feeling into a valentine.

I liked putting lace around a heart—like live snowflakes. Often there was still snow around our country schoolhouse on Valentine's Day. The lace was like gentle decorations from above. I knew that valentines and love had to do both with being gentle and with something from above. And something deep inside.

I remember making hearts I could not give away. They weren't good enough. I crumpled them and started over. I knew what that was about. I don't remember ever making a green or yellow heart. Valentines were always red, pink, white.

Years have passed, and the sign of the heart is still important to me. I mark a heart over important ideas I see and hear and write. The heart is a border, a frame, for special thoughts. I sometimes make a heart to sign off notes I write. I have marked hearts in snow and watched them stay throughout winter and melt in spring.

I remember the beat of your hearts when we held each other close. I liked that feeling. I can feel the rhythm of your life against me. Sometimes I see valentines in your looks. I feel them in the things you say and write. I like to get valentine hearts from you.

Hearts are tough, hearts are tender. I don't recall ever pasting an arrow over a valentine. I think I feared it would wound the heart. That's how I felt when I was nine and ten. That feeling has stayed. If I have wounded your heart, forgive me.

I'm drawing a valentine in the sky toward you. Listen: "I love you."

Love, Dad

Fear Itself

Today I felt an old feeling.

Fear. It can come over me with a word, in a second. Fear is isolation, being shut down, cut off, dropped, hurt. I wonder when fear begins

In a Cleveland airport, a father waved good-bye to his wife and daughter. As he walked across the asphalt to board the plane, his daughter's face pressed against the frosted window of the terminal. The plane door shut. The child cried: "Daddy, Daddy, Daddy!" It was a frightened shout. When she had cried through the fear, she left clinging to her mother. They would be back to see the 747 door open, to see the father step down to join them. I can hear the child then: "Daddy, Daddy, Daddy!" She will understand that her father did not disappear for good. Her fear will go away.

When a fear comes to you, isolate it and name it out loud.

I often felt fear when my parents returned at dark over a narrow country bridge near our home. The bridge had no railings; its planks creaked. The creek looked deep when I was little. I waited for Mom and Dad, staring out a window, wishing them home safe. I followed the headlights of every distant car. I clung to that fear. I did not know the bridge was safe.

I felt an awful fear at nine when Loretta opened our door and said, "He's hurt, he's dead." He was my brother. I was nine. That feeling of fear is old in me—fear of separation, of being cut off, let down, of being alone. Fear stayed in me and grew. It is ancient.

A few years later I heard President Roosevelt saying in a Fireside Chat, "The only thing we have to fear is fear itself." The words stayed with me.

Fear is healed in relationship. Being part of family heals fear. I needed a lot of family love to cast out the fears that had grown inside me. My fear lived to know you, and you helped cast out that fear.

I felt fear when a Gypsy wagon rode past our house in Daykin, population 140. I'd heard stories: I could be stolen from my parents. I made a fear-filled decision: Gypsy means enemy. Fear does not welcome understanding. Fear trusts a liar.

Italians, Greeks, Bohemians, atheists, Jews, Japanese. They were not people I yet knew. I heard rumors, stories; I felt threatened. Because I did not know them, I knew fear.

A Jewish doctor became our family doctor, a healer to us. We knew him, we learned to love him. I visited his synagogue on Fridays. In Newport, a rabbi chaplain gave me his grandfather's prayer shawl. Ten times I placed stone flowers on Jewish graves in Prague. The fear is gone.

I feared Slovaks, Poles, Russians. I did not know them. I slept in camps where they had been war refugees. I met Pomersbach, a Polish refugee. I heard his stories, saw pictures of his mother, learned from him to eat European-style. I watched Polish children snuggle in their parents' laps. What had I to fear but fear itself?

We visited Gypsy memorials in death camps, felt their tears, saw scrapbooks of Roma culture, crafts, song. I heard a Gypsy lecture. I saw a Gypsy dance, bought a necklace made of silver. Why had I been afraid?

I sat inside a Japanese professor's home, drank tea with him, heard him talk about a war he hated, how Tokyo had burned. He showed me a book on Jesus Christ through Japanese eyes. I hugged a woman dressed in a kimono, who married my son. I bathed in a *sento*—a public bath—felt reverence in a washing room. Love was casting out fear. How did fear slip into my vocabulary?

Martha survived four years in the Auschwitz death camp. She was not bitter; there was no fear, no hatred, in her. In a Polish nursing home we sang "Silent Night." Martha, almost blind, recognized our song and my presence. She reached out to dance. We danced "Silent Night." She helped cast out my fear.

You, too, have met my fear. Your love has helped cast it out.

Love, Dad

Holding Hands

How are your hands?

I sometimes check my hands to see my heart. My hands signal my spirit; they tell me if I am stressed, relaxed, loose, tight. When you were little, we held hands. Holding hands I could tell your feelings through your fingers—how tightly you held on, the times when you tried to pull away, the reason why you let go. You could do the same with me.

When you were little, I also began to read the signals in my own hands. I was taught exercises that opened the tips of my fingers and my toes, in which I often felt energy flow through me. You helped me with these exercises as we stood side by side, bending, stretching, imaging, doing deep breathing. There are soul exercises through which I still do this.

We are miles apart, but we can still touch hands.

Look at your hands; fold them in reverence, in prayer. Fold them as a little child, in a bedtime prayer. (We did this together, then we slept.) Now fold them together as though locked in a prison, stranded, helpless. Squeeze them tightly together. Release them slowly, slowly, relaxing. Stretch them open, open, released, freed, tingling. (We did this when we woke.)

How are your hands? I remember when a homemade firecracker blew off two of your fingertips. That's when you really learned to play guitar. You have great hands.

How much we gave each other by hand. Cup your fingers together, as though holding a gift. Look inside your hands and see a gift you received from each other that you still have. Feel the weight of the gift. See the value of the gift you hold. Show the gift to someone. Give the gift to another. Pour out your gift, all of it. Give it all away, be empty-handed.

Open your hands wide. Make them large to collect gifts, to gather gifts, to hold gifts. Pretend with me, for we are so far apart.

In your cupped hands, hold a butterfly without harming its wings. Only let it touch you. See the markings, enjoy it close-up. See it again. Memorize its intricate beauty. Let it go. Watch it fly. You did this with me years ago. Remember?

With your hands, recapture the joy in you, around you, behind you, ahead of you. Hands are near our feelings, near our fears and laughter. Let your hands be glad, waving, painting the sky, swimming through water, holding another hand, swinging, turning pages of a story you want to read again. Let your hands fall, resting, relaxed, open, feeling the peace of your whole body. That is how you rested when we came in to pull nighttime covers to your chin. I kissed you then. I am not too old or too far away to kiss you now.

If you feel pain, hold my hands—like we did then. Let me again share pain with you. Sometimes I will open my pain to you. Feel your hands, see your hands in a storm coming, a storm inside yourself. Let your hands be fearful. Let your hands be afraid as your heart is sometimes afraid. Press them tight. Feel stress in all your fingers, in the clenching, in the pressing. Slowly let the fear go. Release the stress very slowly. Notice your face relaxing with your fingers. Open them suddenly and feel energy flow through them. Close them tight as before; slowly open them, more and more slowly. Feel all the energy flow slowly from you into me, from your hands into mine. Feel how connected your hands are to mine. How often we hugged each other, held each other, clasped hands. We are miles apart, but we can do it again, in this way. What we are doing is real.

This is my wish for you in this letter. Feel how it feels in your hands to receive from another person, to give to another person, to listen, to touch, to do for another, be with one another.

Let your hands show you how we love each other with thoughts, hearts, hands.

Love, Dad

Healing Music

Music is a healer. The CD player you gave me is like medicine.

How many songs do you know by heart? Remember songs, feel them, hum them, tap your feet to their beat. Music heals. Music makes smiles.

My early country life was full of music—or so it seems now. I filled years with humming, singing spirituals, feeling music. On Sundays I joined full force in old hymns led by a pump organ and a congregation of thankful farmers. "Wings Over Jordan," a radio choir, helped make my early Sundays holy. Mother hummed songs when any of us were sick. I cleaned our country church pews while singing all rhythms to my dusting cloth. I worked better when singing, I was better.

We sang as we played when you were little. It was a glad time, like wrens in April. We rocked you to tunes of the Fifties. We rolled toy balls while singing "How Much Is that Doggie in the Window?" Nursery songs were special to you, as was "Jesus Loves Me." You flew and sang with Mary Poppins. You sang along with Howdy Doody. Your tan plastic record player was always warm; you played it over and over each day. You learned to change records yourself. You played and swayed and dreamed and danced all through your childhood years. You embraced music: piano, guitar, organ, clarinet, saxophone, trumpet, violin, harmonica, cello, autoharp, oboe, English horn, drums, bass, kazoo.

The Beatles transformed your world into sounds of music. Issues were given tunes. Human rights were recorded as lyrics. You led peace and justice themes in your own adolescent bands, "Saragon" and "Boa." When did you learn to love Brahms, Mahler, Bach, Mozart, Sibelius?

Rhythm, good lyrics, old tunes heal. Handel's "Alleluia Chorus" and Paul Gerhardt's "Now Rest beneath Night's Shadow" make millions well. Old Testament Psalms were songs to heal, forgive, excite, comfort. Psalms were danced, shouted, wept, chanted, marched. One stanza inside Psalm 13 is a lullaby.

I have calmed and quieted my soul,
like a weaned child with its mother;
my soul within me is like a weaned child.

I wrote a song on a flight to Madison, Wisconsin: "Wrap a Light around My Soul." It was sung and loved. Many found it to be medicine. Give it another tune. Let it be medicine from me to you.

Lord, my Lord, show me your setting sun
that I may know the work you've done,
then wrap a light around my soul
to make me quiet, make me whole.

Lord, my Lord, send me your evening star,
that I may know where angels are,
then wrap a light around my soul
to make me quiet, make me whole.

Lord, my Lord, show me your harvest moon,
when sun is down and work is done,
then wrap a light around my soul
to make me quiet, make me whole.

Lord, my Lord, send me your deepest night,
surprise me with your brightest light,
then wrap a light around my soul
to make me quiet, make me whole.

Lord, my Lord, show me your sudden dawn

when night and dark and sleep are gone,
then wrap a light around my soul
to make me quiet, make me whole.

Lord, my Lord, give me eternal light
then no more tears and no more night,
then wrap your light around my soul
to make me blessed, make me whole.

Love, Dad

I have faith in you . . .

I cannot imagine our home without Bible stories of God.
You liked it best when I lay near you, told stories in my own words,
and asked questions. We talked about news and family affairs
as God's business. God came close at bedtime. When we tucked you in,
I saw the world of children; we were all somehow inside the Bible stories.

To Reflect God's Light

Sometimes I saw your haloes.

As your father, I noticed a light over you, on your faces, in your eyes. It was brighter than sunlight, and it kept an afterglow. I was your father, and what I saw is the truth.

We liked all the festivals of the year: Easter, Pentecost, Thanksgiving, Christmas. We celebrated them all with lights. The festival we celebrated unofficially was the Transfiguration. That's when Jesus shone with light, and the brightness shone through his garments. His body was covered with a halo.

You know the story. Jesus went to a mountaintop with Peter, James, and John; and Moses and Elijah appeared to them in a vision. After this remarkable summit meeting, the disciples wanted to stay on the mountain. What must have appealed to them most was the bright halo illuminating from Jesus. The brightness was greater, I am sure, but somewhat like the haloes I saw in you when you told certain stories, when you brought home an injured horned owl wrapped in your jacket, when the snake birthed eleven babies before your eyes. There are times of brightness and radiation from you I will always remember.

I believe I saw your brightness when your teenage band jammed and all five instruments were in sync. You must have felt the bright harmony, too. You were covered with awe when we watched the northern lights flash in Indiana, and the night sky danced to their rhythm. I saw a halo over you when you looked at a newborn sibling for the first time.

When did you see my light? Was it when I woke you with questions that made you glad to meet the new day? Was it when I waved back during a concert where you were playing oboe or cello? Did you see my halo light when you were thirteen and I introduced you as my colleague in the Astrodome, to a convention of 25,000?

Did you feel a light flow from me when we held you in water and marked God's sign and name on you? Did we see each other's light shine through when we were lost and found each other?

You sometimes reflected God's light when I was looking the other way. You woke with a dream only God's angel could bring, and I did not hear you. I was so proud of a speech you gave, and someone sidetracked me before I could tell you. Your eyes were on fire with love, and I wondered if the lover was right for you.

How many times have we missed God's light in each other?

I am older now, and when the light is right my thin hair glows. It may be your brightness shining through my memory. Many of my brightest times are in the dark, in the quiet of early mornings, when the moon is marking earth shadows, when my heart feels full of stardust. I am sometimes so filled with God's light I feel vibrations of music and rhymes in me, and images that are like medieval paintings of saints. Sometimes I imagine no brighter halo in heaven.

Haloes are often painted over those who are saintly and humble. I believe God's halo is over me most clearly when I am humbled by who you have grown to be, by the possibilities of what you will become, and by what I will never know about you.

You put haloes on me when you light up.

Love, Dad

To Live Up to Your Name

Your names are special.

We carefully chose your names. We said them aloud, looked up their meanings, imagined repeating them for years, looked at you when we said them, wondered how the name would feel to you. Through the years, when I used your name, calling you or addressing you or writing to you, a wonderful feeling came over me. You have a name. Your name is part of who you are, part of who we are together.

This is what baptism means to me. It's a naming time. It reminds us of our larger family name. In this letter I will remember two unusual baptism times in my life. Special ones. I don't think I've told you about these. I like them because they are about emergencies, when we do what we truly believe.

Curtis was sixteen, a member of my church. He once went with me on a parish visit. I wanted him to see the excitement of my work. I liked the spirit of our congregation. It was the fifties, the height of Elvis Presley. Curtis did a perfect imitation of Elvis, which we loved. Curtis and I made a house call. A member of the parish opened the door, and she was crying. Edna took us to a back room where her ninety-nine-year-old uncle was bedfast. He wanted baptism. He wanted the name of God on himself, the sign of the cross over him. He had liked his own name for all these ninety-nine years. But now he wanted to be called Christian. He and the family wanted the name said aloud, in a ritual.

There was water, the Bible, Curtis, and this man who wanted God's name. Curtis stood as his godfather. We gave the old man his new name. Happiness spread over his ninety-nine-year-old body. I remember how Curtis smiled.

We named each of you carefully. We like each of your names: Mark, Beth, Jon, Chris. You share your name with the Gospel writer; your name means "house of God;" your name, "love from God;" yours, "bearer of Christ." In the names we gave you, you were to know you belonged to more than our family. In your baptisms, you took on the name of Christian; you became a brother and sister to the world.

Not long ago we knew of an infant who was critically ill, who had not yet been baptized. I wished the name of God on that child. The infant was twelve miles north of our home. In our shower at home, I faced the hospital. I named the infant, and with much water I marked the sign of God on his breast and brow from a distance. This is a way of life I believe in; it was my secret with God.

Why is baptism so important to me? Why do I mark the sign of a loving cross on planes flying overhead, on trees, over loved ones? I believe we are God's. The sign of the cross is a family emblem in a large world.

Many years ago, Martin Luther said, "I am baptized." Not "I was baptized," or "I have been baptized." He said, "I *am* baptized." Baptism is not something in our past. It has to do with who I am today, who we are, how we are whose we are.

Baptism makes us related in God's family for all times. It completes a family name. Being baptized does not make me better than anyone else; rather, it gives me responsibility, a mission, it ties me to the universe. It helps me know who I am.

I like your names. Your names tell me who you are.

Love, Dad

To Stir My Admiration

It's important to be admired.

Yesterday I saw 30,000 people pay tribute to a person for one hour. That's a lot of admiration.

Today I admire you for your words to one another. You phoned and felt one another's pain. You were not afraid to embrace the hurt which your siblings felt. You reached out and listened, you spoke softly, you assured. You thanked each other, laughed a little, and took heart. It was like Valentine's Day. You gave each other a heart.

Admiration is something like adoration. Something happens so special we become speechless, full of wonder, awestruck. I am that way around you at times.

In the Bible I admired Abraham. I couldn't believe that a father would make such a great sacrifice as to give up his own son, Isaac. I was glad for Isaac being saved; I felt sorry for the ram. I admired Joseph, that he could forgive his brothers who had sold him to strangers. I admired the teenager Mary for believing God's Son would be born of her. I admired Hannah for leaving her young son Samuel in Jerusalem to become an acolyte in the temple. I admired Judas for coming back and throwing down the money he got for betraying Jesus.

I admired a boy who wanted his people to read the Bible in their own language, and who translated God's word into German so they could. His name—Martin Luther. I admired the Wesley brothers in England who could write so many hymns that are so good and that have lived so long. I admired the champion Joe Louis for saying hello to his mother after every fight.

You are all so different, but you know one another's gifts. For being so far apart—so different—you stayed close. When you were little, you sat close at the table and pasted valentines together. You still paste valentines together. Fathers like closeness.

Last night I listened to a J. S. Bach recording. I rocked and watched the February moon move through the western sky at midnight. Deer roamed our yard, hungry this winter. I admired the beauty of that darkness, the light of that moon, the architect who designed this room with ten windows in the roof to welcome the night sky. At night especially my admiration turns to adoration.

I was filled with admiration twenty-four years ago when attending a junior high band concert. You were in the oboe chair. The band dressed in red and white looked like a checkerboard on stage. I admired all the players. (Once upon a time I wanted to learn saxophone. Instead, I drove home to do chores.) Then came the highest admiration. A virtuoso, violin tucked under his chin, stood to play. There was a hush in the room; we all stared with admiration as he began to play. He played two measures, heard a string out of tune, stopped. He stopped to tune. Everyone saw him do it, waited, heard it happen. You saw, too. He began again, violin in tune. There was a huge ovation when he finished. I admired that moment, that man, his message. A virtuoso started over to do it right.

I admired you when you trudged through deep snow to a rabbit hutch to feed Miranda, to give her warm water in winter. I admired that you practiced piano in front of us, got it right, were not embarrassed by the family being there. I admired when, at Christmastime in a restaurant, you talked with me about a fear I feel. The fear will heal in me now. I admired that when a marriage did not work, you did not give up loving and caring; you keep alive a passion and joy for life. I admire that you have traveled far each year to be with us on a holiday, to keep family rituals and love alive. I admire you for composing a new tune and lyrics to match—writing so each note and word is right. I admire you when you edit my writing, to help me say it so it fits the reader. I like when you look at me without saying anything, and we know what it means.

Adoration and admiration are so very close. We give these to God. We give these to each other. I admire you.

Love, Dad

To Pray with Me

You asked me, "Do you pray for the dead?"

Only twice in seventy years have I touched someone dead. The first time, when I was nine; the second time, last week. Two times in seventy years. Both times I was sure: the person is still alive, but not living in the body. Near yet not near.

I still feel my brother's cool skin on me. The wake was in the northwest corner of our country house, the parlor. The room was cold, so was my brother. I knew Paul's new place was near and far at once. Being near and far at once was now no problem for Paul. That I believed.

Last week I touched a baby who had died. I feel the cold on my palms now. Ethan was not in that body, but he was in the room — and distant at once. My belief has stayed the same for sixty years.

Do I pray for Paul, for Ethan? Yes. Both are part of my life. In cathedrals of Europe we saw paintings of large families. Some family members have a white cloth over their mouth. They are silent, they are the dead. But they remain members of the family; they still count. They are in the family photo, in the album, in the story.

I think of dead persons I once knew. I still know them. I was with them until the grave. I stood at the fresh grave mound. They stayed near and far at once. They have more space now for living. I have seen mothers and fathers whisper at graves — sometimes to the loved ones who have died, sometimes to God, sometimes to themselves. These are all the same. Prayer places us into the enormous, intimate space and time of God. Life is not so much a line but a circle. Life line is limiting.

Prayer. It is direct, indirect; a mood, a want, an anger, a hope, a cry. Do I pray for the dead? Yes, and I pray with them and through them and among them. So I am closer to God. They are alive in God's space.

Sometimes I talk to you in silence when we are thousands of miles apart. I repeat words you say, your tone of voice. You are alive in me. Help me stay open to your questions about death. Help my God circle grow.

I do not believe the dead cease to exist, become useless. I talked with Pastor Dan and his church about saints in their cemetery. We told good stories, faith stories. The faith of the saints lives in the living. I asked, "Are they still active members?" Pastor Dan and his congregation counted tombstones and doubled the church's membership in an hour.

After country funerals in my father's church, people stayed, ate, drank, rested before long drives home. I remember their stories, laughing, tears, loving. It was a loud time, a time of living. The dead seemed very much alive.

Pastor Rudy asked me to make a speech at his wife's funeral. She had composed music to my lyrics, so he said: "You know her." I heard the Bible text about mansions in heaven, and Jesus preparing places for all of us. When it was my turn, I said, "Rudy, where is she? Where are those rooms, those mansions? Is one room in your mind?" He touched his head and shouted, "Yes." I asked the question in other ways. Rudy's family claimed some of heaven's rooms in their own minds, their own memories. That made eighteen rooms. Professors and students came up to me later and said it was true for them, too. Pastor Rudy's wife lived on in more than three hundred heavenly rooms.

Do I pray for the dead? Saints are in my prayers. They influence me, inspire me, cheer me on. Scripture says that heavenly hosts are a cheering section. Sometimes I hear them.

Mystics believe everything is on God's Web Line. Keep asking me questions. Help my faith continue to grow.

Love, Dad

To Wait for Easter

May I tell you about my Easter?

You are not here. I want to remember this Easter night as if I were with you.

Saturday evening, the Easter vigil. The sanctuary is in shadows, and we are here together. Christ rises in the dark, before dawn. In this dark I feel an Easter I knew when I was little; it is still alive in me. What in this night of mine will be a good inheritance for you?

One candle lights this large room. The shadows are dark as the ones I knew in my bedroom when I was a boy in Nebraska. Tomorrow is Easter. I am in a darkened sanctuary with a single candle, waiting for Easter. Candles slow me down. Waiting for Easter took a long time when I was little. It started at the end of Good Friday, went slowly through Silent Saturday, and finally into Easter. Thank goodness, thank God.

In these long years I have waited often: waited for meetings, for persons, for places, for times. I have waited wildly, impatiently, wondering, looking on tiptoe. I cannot imagine a life that does not know waiting, impatient expecting.

I waited for you to come home from school, from vacation, from a party. Patient waiting was something I struggled to learn, prayed about. I waited for you to heal, to pass an exam, to tell me something on your own. Waiting was a matter of timing, and time is half of life.

Silent Saturday was the slow time between Good Friday and Easter, the day we talked in a whisper, walked on tiptoe, played softly, waited. We felt our way through the day as if in the dark. That's what I'm feeling tonight with one candle lighted in this darkened sanctuary. I am young again, hopeful, waiting in a darkened place.

On Silent Saturday, young Herbert Brokering could have told you why the graves on the country hilltop lay in one direction, facing east. If tomorrow would be Resurrection Day, all 210 saints in our Nebraska St. James Cemetery would sit up, stand up, face the rising sun, face the east, face Jerusalem. Face a new heaven and earth. That is a quiet thought inside me tonight.

Childhood Easter was for me a nest of dry grass that I made and hid, to be hunted and found by an Easter rabbit. How carefully, on Saturday, I formed a nest in a sacred place, so no gust of wind would harm the soft pocket I'd molded with my child fist. If it needed to be bigger for more eggs, I made the pocket with two fists. So well did I hide the nest, that I could only hope it would be found. In me on Silent Saturday was a hope and a knowing, both at once. It was like my faith. I both hoped and believed the nest would be found. I do not remember it was ever missed.

During Holy Week, families came to smooth graves with fresh earth. People came to rake, plant flowers, trim grass. Graves were ready for Easter, ready to be visited, prayed beside, talked about, perhaps opened by angels. Maybe. We never knew. The hilltop still looks hopeful on this Silent Saturday evening.

Some grave vaults were made of steel, some of cement. I heard farmers talk about lifetime warrantees on new grave vaults. They were air-tight, waterproof, guaranteed. I marveled. I knew at the Resurrection earth would open, lids of steel vaults would come off. Their guarantee was not against Easter.

Earlier today I found a violet under the melting snow. It will bloom very soon unless there is an April freeze. Some grass is green under the snow.

The candle seems brighter now. My eyes can see more clearly. You feel very close to me this Easter vigil.

Love, Dad

To Make Me Safe

We need each other to feel safe.

When you were learning to walk, you sometimes kept your eyes on your feet and the floor. Then you fell. We stood before you, smiling, calling your name, our arms outstretched. When you kept your eyes on us, you felt safe, and you didn't fall. Many times I keep my eyes on you and I feel safe.

After heart surgery I walked the street in the valley of our home. When I felt anxious, I held one of you before my eyes. I saw you, felt you, heard you cheer me with a soft sentence. It was what I needed to feel safe. Often I have done this. As you kept your eyes on me while learning to walk the distance of a room, so I now keep my ear tuned to your voice in order to walk the distance before me. We need each other to be safe.

Once there was a rash of airline accidents. Planes were crashing; many people feared flying. When walking onto a plane, I saw ahead of me a famous professor, loved and admired by the whole church. I was far behind; he did not see me. But in seeing him, I felt safer boarding the flight. After we were airborne I looked back. The professor had an aisle seat; he was sound asleep and unworried. I was sure we'd make it.

I took a stress test fifteen years ago, which I somehow feared. A chaplain came in the night to my hospital bed, pressed his finger to my brow, and said, "Stay there." I have felt that spot on my brow many times since he touched it. I have thought about his words. The spot was where water and a word signed me in baptism. It's where I feel centered. It's where I feel special. This is the spot where ashes have been marked on me during Lent. In times of stress, I touch my forehead, see that chaplain again, hear his words, feel his touch, feel the cross on my brow—and feel safe.

In Prague I heard a professor tell of his faith. He told about how, during all the time he lived in danger of sinking in an atheistic system, he kept his eyes on Jesus. He walked the stormy waters unafraid. He said, "I knew I'd go under, as did Peter, if I looked down at my own two feet. I kept my eyes on Jesus, and I walked on water those thirty years." He is someone I wish you could meet.

It is not enough to keep our eyes on ourselves.

In Leipzig I walked with 180,000 in a march for peace. Coffins were brought to the city in case violence erupted. Many feared the danger but marched anyway. I saw a ninety-year-old man I knew, and I kept my eye on him. He had been singing before entering the crowd; he carried a candle. There was no fear or anger in him. He calmed those around me, and he calmed me. There were others like him who calmed the thousands. No weapon was shot, no one was hurt. People spoke their feelings, lighted candles, held hands, and went home. The old man had been a pastor under Hitler, Stalin, and Hoenicker. He was not afraid. He was not afraid of the water under him. He kept his eyes on Jesus.

Remember times when you were little and afraid? Suddenly you saw your mother or me. We saw each other. You smiled. The tears dried quickly. We both felt safer because we were together.

Sometimes I phone you when I feel afraid. To hear your voice is enough. I am brave again.

We have each other to feel safe. Keep your eyes on someone who makes you feel safe.

Love, Dad

To See God

Where is God in a family?

Where was God in our family when you were still living in our house, when you were part of our coming and going? I thought back to the places God could be found in our home.

God was in your eyes. In your eyes I looked for God's mysteries. In your eyes I could see a universe like none other, a universe that was all your own. God had given you insights of your own, ideas and understandings that were wondrous and deep. In your eyes I felt near God in our family.

I found God's places when you told what happened in your day—how it felt to fall, what the owl looked like, who walked home with you. I saw God in the spaces where you lived, in the tiny times of your day. I saw God most real in our home in you.

I knew God's nearness when your face was full of wonder, your eyes were encyclopedias of information. You could not tell it all, some of it never will be said. Your face showed me you stood in some holy of holies; I could not go there. You were in God's presence. I felt a light between us.

I cannot imagine our home without Bible stories about God. You did not always want a reading at the dinner table. You liked it best when I lay near you on the rug, told the stories in my own words, and asked questions. A large flipchart on the wall made stories, people, places, more real. I felt God near when we prayed at each meal. We talked about news and family affairs as God's business. God came closest at bedtime. When we tucked you in, I saw the world of children, and we were all somehow inside the Bible stories.

Sometimes I wanted one more sign of faith from you, and you already believed. I wrestled with a God who went with you on hikes, who watched you climb high watertowers, and wiggled with you across a river of ice. In the risks and escapades of my family I knew God's nearness, saw God's presence.

Holy days of the church year were family benchmarks. We celebrated with special meals, gifts, seasonal games, costumes, cakes, and candles. Our house was like church. We blessed rooms, trees, people. We welded scrap metal into holy signs, a broken hay fork cast shadows we named Calvary. Driftwood crucifixes hung on our walls. We talked about these things as we talked about sledding, trolls, picnics, and parades. All things were holy; God was in all things. Our house sometimes was a church. We called these worship times with friends "House Church." Candelabra and crosses were set on tables, bread and wine were served from kitchen counters, and we heard church words spoken, preached, and prayed in our houses. Families sat close wherever there was room. Babies were passed around like teddy bears. Houses became sanctuaries, and our family felt bigger. Each room felt like a room God knew.

God was near in the night when you woke with fear and called for help, when it was dark and I did not know if you were safe. God also came when I worried, and you were just fine, laughing at some good party, playing in a dance band, talking with a friend in some place you liked. Had I trusted God more, I would have seen God more, and trusted you more. God helped me through dark and worrisome storms. God was bailing me out while you were having a ball.

Where is God in a family? In so many, many places. God is in a word spoken, a word heard, a gesture, a touch, a dream, a hurt, a good-bye, a new song. God's Spirit is in the family spirit, mood, attitude. God is present in truth spoken, in love shared, in need shown, in seasons unfolding, in tiny times.

We are to be eyewitnesses to God. Perhaps that is what we learned together in our young family years. God is present in the comings and goings, and in all times between.

Love, Dad

To Teach Me

What is a father?

In your beginning, I thought I'd be a father because that's what happens when people marry. We'd make love and soon you'd be there.

I thought being a father was something like cloning. There'd be new people on earth who looked like your mother and me — who, in many ways, would be like us. When I'd die, they'd go on living, and that would keep me alive longer. That was my picture of being a father.

Being a father was a little like being God. Two people could make something in their own image that no one else could duplicate. Being a father would be like placing another Adam and Eve on earth. Being a little like God was awesome, so I felt very special.

Being a father was having a chance to do for your children what you wish your father had done for you. I could give what I didn't get to have. I'd be sure my children got music lessons, that they could swim and dance. I'd play with them and have time to listen.

Being a father was having a chance to do for your children all the good things your father did do for you. We'd make things with hammers and nails and build tree houses the way my father and I had done.

I'd tell my children all I knew about God, as my father did for me. I'd surely hold them on my lap and show them how much I loved them, as my mother had done with me.

I'd give my children what I got and what I missed. Being father was like another chance for me to live. Sometimes it scared me.

Being father was a risk because there's always a war that wants children to grow up and fight. I looked at each of you and prayed you would be safe — especially from a battlefield.

As a father I'd give my children my faith. We'd grow together to believe the same things about God, and I'd tell them important things to know about going to heaven forever. That's what I wanted most of all—that we'd spend forever together plus a long time on earth.

But you are not clones. And I am not very much like God. I did not do all the things I wanted to do with you. I have not heard most of your stories. Your faith is not like mine. I soon learned that a child grows to be a person. You grow in ways unpredictable. You chose different options than I did.

As years went on, I often found myself wanting to be like you, to be cloned in some ways in your image. You were recreating your father. I was growing in your image. That felt good to me; I was learning to be a new creation.

I began to hear words not in my vocabulary. You spoke images and sang words that were of another world; I could not always catch the meanings. You sang through wars and marches; you sang justice and peace lyrics I could not always hear between rock sounds. I was understanding a first line of a stanza when you were on the next song. I worried what all these words were doing in you, to you. I was not in charge. You were showing me how to grow in thought and feeling—your way.

While I was reviewing stories of Joseph and Jesus and Mary and Sarah in the Bible, you were memorizing songs by Peter, Paul, and Mary, and the Beatles. Some of your songs were like some of my hymns. You bridged a gap between secular and sacred. My life grew more special, healthier, because of you. I looked at the Bible and you learned the world. We shared what we'd learned, questions we had. Our answers came out nearly the same. Sometimes I was afraid of what you did not know or believe. Sometimes I was afraid of what I did not believe or know. I sometimes feared for myself more than for you.

Being your father I could not play God the Father. At best I could be a child of God with you.

It is a risk to birth a child. It is a risk for a child to have a parent. What a chance we have taken, you and I—the chance of a lifetime.

When God birthed the earth it was recorded, "Behold, it was very good." That's how I feel about you. When you were born, I looked on you and hoped to spend forever together. I'm still counting on it.

Love, Dad

Because God Has Faith in You

God has faith in you.

These letters are about faith for they are about God. Faith is the bottom line of all the letters. What is faith? I knew faith when I was very little. Faith was what my mother felt toward me. I knew her faith in me, I lived in the joy of her faith. My faith was a response to hers; it was not separate from that of my mother.

Father carried me high on his shoulders. He knew he could hold me; I knew I wouldn't fall. I believed in him; my confidence in him held me. My faith was in my father. We do not have faith apart from someone else.

From Father and Mother I learned stories of God. God made me and all that exists; God wants me to grow, to love, to be wise, to be perfect. God is my biggest fan club, my greatest support. God goes all out to make me safe, love me, and give me life. God believes in me; and when I believe this, I believe in God. My faith begins with God's faith in me.

Faith is a two-way street between me and God, me and others. My faith acts on God's faith. I remember the Bible verse that goes: "We love God because God first loved us." I felt love early in life, when sitting on Mother's lap, when riding Dad's shoulders. They loved me; and when I believed this, then I loved them back.

Early I learned that Lutherans had faith. I thought I had a Lutheran faith, it was the right faith—the best faith, that's why we had it. More and more, faith became something I had on my own, something I had to be sure I wouldn't lose. It was like a right answer that had to be kept up-to-date so it would stay true. I could look at it, define it, prove it, and confess it by heart. I learned to protect it. I felt sorry others didn't have this faith. I prayed I would keep it and they would get it. Faith had more to do with something I did than with God's faith in me. The two got disconnected.

I would have to find mother's faith again.

I studied Luther, lived in his cities. I wanted to document Luther's faith. I discovered Luther was a Catholic, a Christian, and not a Lutheran. He talked about faith as God's faith toward him. Luther's faith was not his own; it was God's, shown through Jesus.

Good. Then I would have a Christian faith. But I found that Jesus was a Jew who never called himself a Christian. He got faith from God. He had the will and mind and love of God, so closely were they connected. Jesus was in God and God was in Jesus. Faith ran back and forth like a yo-yo, like a closed circuit, like my mother and me. Jesus talked about knowing the Father and the Father knowing him, and them being in each other. Faith was close as a branch is to its vine.

Now I realized: Jesus was not a Lutheran or a Christian, Jesus was in God, from God, of God. The faith Jesus knew was God's faith. The love Jesus knew was God's love. Now I was back home, in my beginning, in Mother's lap, on Dad's shoulders.

So it was when I was little. My faith came from someone's faith in me. Faith begets faith. I like the thought: God has faith—God believes—in me. That makes it possible for me to believe in God, and in myself. And in others.

Dr. Lawrence Little told my graduate class that Jesus' prayer was for all people. The Lord's Prayer is a prayer for anyone believing in God, a prayer for the world, all religions, all persons. It dawned on me: God's faith is for all creation. God believes in every created human being.

I write you letters of faith, letters out of God's faith in me.

Faith is like a yo-yo. The yo-yo goes out and comes back on the same string. There is one faith; it comes from God and it returns to God. God believes in us; we believe in God.

And because God believes in us, we can believe in each other. We have God's faith in us. I have faith in you.

Love, Dad

Printed in the United States
111081LV00002B/22-45/A